"Leadership is mission critical, especially in a storm. My friend Bishop Geoffrey Dudley draws from his vast life experiences in ministry, the military, academia, and relationships in writing *Leading Through Storms*. No easy platitudes, only well-earned wisdom in multiple storms distilled into pragmatic, actionable steps. You'll understand yourself and your storm and come out stronger."

Sam Chand, leadership consultant and author of *Leadership Pain: The Classroom for Growth*

"*Leading Through Storms* is unlike any other leadership book I have read. It takes us through the trenches, walking us along the realistic path of struggle as we attempt to lead amid challenges and uncertainty. Bishop Dudley shares from the heart while helping us to stand firm even as waves of doubt crash around us. This book is for everyone. Highly recommended."

Michael O. Emerson, Chavanne fellow in religion and public policy at Rice University in Houston, Texas, and coauthor of *Divided by Faith*

"This is a powerful leadership book marinated in a painful personal narrative. It is well-crafted, helpful, and honest. It is also raw, compelling, and unsettling. But most of all, it is intrinsically hopeful."

Shane L. Bishop, senior pastor of Christ Church in Fairview Heights, Illinois, and author of *That's Good News*

"It is an honor to compose this endorsement for *Leading Through Storms* by Bishop Geoffrey V. Dudley. My acquaintance with Bishop Dudley since 1993 has profoundly influenced my family and the church my wife and I lead. Throughout the previous seventeen years, we have observed his adeptness in overcoming adversities. His candor in this book, especially regarding the challenges faced in ministry, provides essential insights for all leaders. Bishop Dudley's narrative exhibits transformational leadership and serves as an essential guide for individuals confronting the challenges of pastoral life."

Mack L. McCullough, senior pastor at Word in Season Ministries

"Bishop Dudley captures the essence of academia and application of leadership development theories by using his real-life narrative as the lens by which *Leading Through Storms* causes you to view leadership. He puts the theories of leadership in the test tube of the challenges of ministry, and with each chapter, the Bunsen burner is turned up, and the reader learns how to lead himself or herself and to inspire their followers to accomplish the vision of the church."

Joshua D. Henson, associate professor, chair of graduate studies, and director of the MBA program at Southeastern University in Lakeland, Florida

"Bishop Dudley skillfully uncovers the inequities in the church financial world leading to the excessive stress that senior pastors, especially those of color, must navigate in order to serve their communities. Not only does he expose the racism in the financial space, he survived it to tell about it and give hope and a framework to help others through the minefield of church construction. Read this book so you can walk in the boardroom ready to negotiate and ready to lead in the pulpit."
Kenneth Lewis, CEO of Clearinghouse Advisory Group Inc.

"There is a plethora of definitions for leadership and thousands of books on shelves in major bookstores. *Leading Through Storms* is a great tool for leaders who are marketplace secular thinkers as well as many who are vital voices in the sacred community. The concept of the core team of our ministries that helps navigate times of uncertain 'space' moments is relevant to current times. Bishop Dudley has merged his scholarly insights and life experiences that prepare every leader for the chaos when people jump ship and to be okay asking for help after the storm!"
Wanda Frazier-Parker, copastor at Truth Tabernacle Ministries

"*Leading Through Storms* is a love letter to every follower of Jesus who understands the call to lead sometimes requires us to lead while limping. Bishop Geoffrey V. Dudley Sr. has provided a masterful show-and-tell guide that seamlessly weaves biblical texts, business acumen, and bold acts of faith to offer kingdom-building principles for those called to leadership in Christ's church. Bishop Dudley's transparency is rare and refreshing. The emotional vulnerability with which he shares the pinnacles and pitfalls of his church-planting journey will provide encouragement to faith-walking leaders for generations to come. I highly recommend this book to everyone who has given God a yes, understanding that giving up with God is never an option."
Traci D. Blackmon, founder and lead consultant at HopeBuilds LLC

"Geoffrey Dudley's *Leading Through Storms* is a deeply personal and practical guide for those considering church ministry and for those already serving churches who might be wondering, *What did I get myself into?* Weaving together his own story and the principles of leadership gleaned from a variety of sources, Dudley offers insights into how leaders can navigate through choppy waters or perhaps avoid some storms altogether. Share *Leading Through Storms* as a blessing to your church staff or with someone you know in seminary."
Dennis Edwards, seminary dean and vice president of church relations at North Park University

"*Leading Through Storms* should be required reading for leaders in ministry, especially new pastors. The challenges are written about in an authentic way that leaves you feeling like Bishop Dudley knows your story and you are not alone. His transparency and vulnerability are rare and a great encouragement."
Angela M. Tate, associate pastor at West Side Missionary Baptist Church in St. Louis, Missouri

"We often define leadership as influence and leave it at that. Rarely do we go deeper into how influence is implemented and executed in the dark days of leadership. *Leading Through Storms* will take the reader on a journey through the emotional struggles of a modern-day Elijah. Bishop Geoffrey Dudley vulnerably shares how he led a church during seemingly insurmountable struggles and utter depression. Through leadership theory, Scripture, praxis, and self-reflection, *Leading Through Storms* gives readers ears to hear and eyes to see how to lead themselves and others out of the storms of life."
T.D. Jakes, founder and senior pastor at The Potter's House

"A standout book for leaders facing the paradox of working with less while aiming to achieve more, who grapple with systemic inequities and face issues requiring new frameworks and fresh thinking! Bishop Geoffrey Dudley addresses these issues with transparency and hard-fought wisdom, exploring ways to balance the demands of leadership with the need for self-care to fulfill God's mandate to love your neighbor as yourself. Reading this book will inspire you to hope again, lead differently, think creatively, and champion a style that's resilient and persevering yet compassionate to self and others."
Dana Carson, president of Kingdom Theological Seminary in Houston, Texas

"Geoffrey Dudley passionately argues that leadership isn't just about theory—it's about practice. He believes that true understanding comes from delving into real-life experiences and uncovering the secrets that distinguish good leadership from bad. According to Dudley, challenging times are both a litmus test for leadership effectiveness and a classroom for strengthening leadership skills.

"In today's rapidly changing world, we need ministers who prioritize the well-being of others and embrace the reality that what worked in the past may not work in the future. It's not just about having good ideas; it's crucial to understand how to make effective decisions in a constantly evolving landscape. While the academic scholarship on leadership theories garners attention, the practical aspect of leadership needs more examination. This book stands out as it seamlessly blends Scripture, leadership scholarship, and real-world experience. Dudley offers a compelling combination of academic rigor, engagement with biblical text, and lived wisdom.

"This book is designed for practitioners who want to enhance their skills with a valuable resource and guide. It goes beyond just offering wise sayings, as it is the result of critical reflection on lived experience and is informed by solid scholarship. The book draws upon Scripture and emphasizes the importance of reflection, contextuality, and people-centered leadership—qualities essential for navigating the complexities of human experience in today's world. The examples and frameworks presented here are practical lessons for those striving to lead better.

"Journey with this scholar-practitioner as he explores the rich terrain of ministry leadership. This combination of insightful scriptural interpretation and practical wisdom is thought provoking and relevant to the challenges faced in today's ministry. Ministry leadership is not just about holding a title or position. It's not just about who we are but also about what we do. Leadership is about how we interact with and influence others. It's about the impact we have on people, the difference we make, and the legacy we leave behind—all for the glory of God!

"This book is an open invitation to embark on a journey, explore, be challenged, and ultimately pave the way for good ministry leadership that is intentional and purposeful."

Antipas L. Harris, president of the Harris Institute and the Urban Renewal Center

FOREWORD BY WALTER SCOTT THOMAS

LEADING THROUGH STORMS

SUCCESSFULLY NAVIGATING MINISTRY WHILE MAINTAINING YOUR MENTAL HEALTH

GEOFFREY V. DUDLEY SR.

An imprint of InterVarsity Press
Downers Grove, Illinois

InterVarsity Press
P.O. Box 1400 | Downers Grove, IL 60515-1426
ivpress.com | email@ivpress.com

©2025 by Geoffrey V. Dudley Sr.

All rights reserved. No part of this book may be reproduced in any form without written permission from InterVarsity Press.

InterVarsity Press® is the publishing division of InterVarsity Christian Fellowship/USA®. For more information, visit intervarsity.org.

All Scripture quotations, unless otherwise indicated, are taken from The Holy Bible, New International Version®, NIV®. Copyright © 1973, 1978, 1984, 2011 by Biblica, Inc.™ Used by permission of Zondervan. All rights reserved worldwide. www.zondervan.com. The "NIV" and "New International Version" are trademarks registered in the United States Patent and Trademark Office by Biblica, Inc.™

While any stories in this book are true, some names and identifying information may have been changed to protect the privacy of individuals.

The publisher cannot verify the accuracy or functionality of website URLs used in this book beyond the date of publication.

Cover design: Faceout Studio, Spencer Fuller
Interior design: Daniel van Loon

ISBN 978-1-5140-0914-7 (print) | ISBN 978-1-5140-0915-4 (digital)

Printed in the United States of America ∞

Library of Congress Cataloging-in-Publication Data
Names: Dudley, Geoffrey V., Sr. author.
Title: Leading through storms : successfully navigating ministry while maintaining your mental health / Geoffrey V. Dudley Sr.
Description: Downers Grove, IL : InterVarsity Press, [2025] | Includes bibliographical references.
Identifiers: LCCN 2024042354 (print) | LCCN 2024042355 (ebook) | ISBN 9781514009147 (paperback) | ISBN 9781514009154 (ebook)
Subjects: LCSH: Clergy–Mental health. | Christian leadership. | Pastoral theology. | Mental health–Religious aspects–Christianity.
Classification: LCC BV4398 .D83 2025 (print) | LCC BV4398 (ebook) | DDC 253/.2–dc23/eng/20241101
LC record available at https://lccn.loc.gov/2024042354
LC ebook record available at https://lccn.loc.gov/2024042355

I would like to dedicate this book to my parents, the late Bishop Leamon Dudley Sr., DD, and the late Ida Dorothy Dudley. They raised me to be the leader that I am today. They instilled qualities to allow me to pursue the purpose on my life with fervor, and I would not be here without their prayers and steadfast love.

CONTENTS

Foreword by Walter Scott Thomas ... 1
Introduction ... 3

PART 1: BEFORE THE STORM

1. Calling: How We Got Here ... 11
2. Core: The Strength of Your Leaders ... 22

PART 2: WEATHER ALERT

3. Consecrated Courage: Prepare for the Storm ... 37
4. Construction: How to Build the Church ... 50
5. Canceled: When People Jump Ship ... 62

PART 3: IN THE STORM

6. Chaos: Multiple Things Can Go Wrong ... 79
7. Cash: When Money Is Not Enough ... 92
8. Community: From "Hosanna!" to "Crucify Him!" ... 107

PART 4: AFTER THE STORM

9. Counseling: It's Okay to Ask for Help ... 117
10. Clarity: How We Made It Over ... 128

Acknowledgments ... 139
Appendix: Self-Assessment Tools ... 141
Notes ... 143

FOREWORD

WALTER SCOTT THOMAS

MINISTRY CHALLENGES ARE INEVITABLE—preparation is intentional! These seven words capture the heart of this transparent and intellectually insightful seminal book on leadership development. Bishop Dudley has taken the highbrow leadership theories of the academy and built a staircase to reaching higher levels of leadership development for everyone who is in ecclesial and organizational leadership. Written with an unparalleled level of honesty, the narrative of his leadership journey is a story that will equip leaders for the storms that arise in ministry, be it megachurch visionary or senior pastor of a storefront church.

With each chapter, Bishop Dudley leads you on a scavenger hunt for more. At the end of each chapter, you find the more you were looking for with the application of the lessons he learned. One may ask the question why the body of Christ needs one more book on leadership development. Indeed, there is a plethora of excellent books on leadership. None, at least, that I am aware of, that invite you into the leader's life and lay bare the mistakes, missteps, strikeouts, and valleys as well as the mountaintop victorious experiences. The bookshelves are full of how-to books that have no real connection to the real world most leaders face. Bishop Dudley's passion for leadership development has inspired him to push past the theories of leadership into the execution of leadership principles. He skillfully balances life experience with academia.

Get ready to level up your leadership skills as you read and apply this book to your context, be it a ministry, nonprofit, or for-profit organization.

INTRODUCTION

SIMON SINEK IS WIDELY CREDITED with helping organizations and individuals discover their "why." Knowing your reason for being, he argues, is critical to fulfilling your purpose in life.[1] The late Dr. Myles Munroe called knowing your why, knowing your purpose. You cannot know what to do with a thing or person if you do not know their purpose.[2]

My why and purpose for writing this book is to take the foreboding Eurocentric models of leadership and leadership development and the overwhelming theoretical research language of organizational leadership and break them down into practical concepts using a narrative. Jesus used storytelling to teach his disciples how to lead and follow and he was the greatest storyteller of all time. His parables drove his points home, leaving both his followers and detractors speechless and informed to live better lives. Western majority culture and the academy often overlook story as legitimate pedagogy despite it being the core learning tool of other cultures. The Bible is the product of an oral tradition and there is no greater leadership text in existence.[3] Too often leadership development is taught from an academic point of view that does not reach the leader in the trenches of leading. Story reaches the trenches because it originates in the trenches.

Additionally, leadership is seen through the lens of great success models of European Americans, which leave others wondering at their seeming failures. These models are portrayed as orthodoxy of leadership and have resources and years of success that others lack. The crucible of leadership is burnished when one has little, is facing a lot, and is asked to do more. There is a need for examples of leadership for those who only have a lot of desire. What emerges from this type of storytelling leadership development is applicable to all.

John Maxwell, arguably the guru of Christian leadership development, presents a particular type of leadership that might best be described as triumphant white evangelicalism: leadership is success, and success is having megachurches (he pastors in a twenty-eight-thousand-member megachurch in Florida), businesses that make lots of money, and the character traits that attract followers in droves. His books are outstanding, but they speak nothing of the realities that *Leading Through Storms* will describe. They are simply not his realities. This absence leaves a gaping hole for the millions of Christians facing a less-than-equal playing field, and for nearly all leaders who will face incredible storms. How can they lead in the face of things going wrong, of being questioned, and while being wronged?

Maxwell's books and others like them focus on contrasting biblical leadership with worldly leadership. They thus examine biblical principles that characterize a Christian leader, often emphasizing the need for leaders to exhibit Christian character and rely on God for wisdom in leading. Every one of these models of leadership development is white, bringing a particular set of experiences into the world they inhabit and practice their leadership. I'm not critiquing this so much as pointing out that both the topic and the author of this book bring something truly unique to the Christian leadership genre.

Although *Leading Through Storms* draws on the wisdom of other books, it details Christian leadership in a much different context and draws out new applications, principles, and understandings. It raises the profile of praxis leadership much like a medical doctor's practice: even with the requisite education, they are still confronted with cases that cause them to reach beyond the books and into their gut to determine how to save a patient in an under-resourced operating room. It is with this type of leadership that many leaders of color, including myself, must pastor, lead, plant churches, and develop them into profiles of courage for the communities they serve.

Finally, I wrote this book to address the mental health of leaders. For far too many, seeking professional therapy remains a stigma.[4] Since Covid-19, the demand for counseling has skyrocketed, especially among African American pastors.[5] Ministry leaders need tools for their mental health as well.[6] By pulling the veil back on my journey, my hope is it to give permission to ministry leaders to do the same. It is hard to lead without spreading your brokenness onto those who follow unless you get help. Ministry storms are certain, and leaders need tools to navigate them without projecting their pain onto their people. Sickness, illness, anxiety, and depression can quickly become a contagion, resulting in a sick and depressed congregation because the leader has not sought help. One would never ignore a broken leg and continue walking on it. Leaders should take the same attitude to leading with an untreated broken spirit.

The purpose of this book is to equip the reader with the leadership skills to ride the waves of ministry through turbulent winds of ministry. I intentionally share my backstory as I believe the transparency will be transformative for the reader. As a good friend of mine who found business success selling high-tech educational services once told me, "Facts tell, stories sell." My story sails on the bipolar winds of success and failure.

The lyrics of the gospel writer and psalmist Douglas Miller best describe my backstory: "Though the storms keep on raging in my life / And sometimes it's hard to tell the night from day."[7] There were many times when I didn't know night from day. There was the night of the incomplete construction project—red iron that greeted me as I drove onto the church campus month after month, year after year. There was the day of another family telling me they were leaving our church in search of another place to worship. There was the twilight of the bank reneging on its loan commitments then threatening foreclosure and calling the loan. Day or night, I couldn't always tell, but I could hear my Old Testament professor ending every lecture with, "Sunday is coming, and you got to preach!"

The demands of leadership do not stop when Mount Carmel experiences turn into running for your life. They only intensify. With each problem comes the opportunity to rejoice in victory or sink in defeat. John Maxwell titled his book *Failing Forward*. The writer of Proverbs said, "Though the righteous fall seven times, they rise again" (24:16). But how do you keep getting up when the fall is further than you could have imagined?

Despite my walking through brokenness week after week, month after month, year after year, I had to preach without, "bleeding on the people," as my homiletics professor would say. In the pages that follow, I detail the storm I had to lead myself out of to lead my church through. Keeping the church and myself upright and afloat was no small task, but with each gale wind the mast and sails withstood the gust and got stronger with leadership skills and precision.

In this book, I detail leadership development skills in bite-sized portions digestible for every type of leader. Each chapter shares my story through the lens of a leadership theory. At the conclusion of each chapter, the leadership theory that is reflected in the narrative of my story is discussed. Then the theory is discussed as lessons learned followed by questions for reflection and discussion for the reader to consider and apply the leadership theory in a person's life.

I believe my experience will provide the reader with a living epistle of how to lead and live in a storm. It is divided into the phases of a storm: "Before the Storm," "Weather Alert," "In the Storm," and "After the Storm."

"Before the Storm" encompasses the history of my calling and leadership development. My thirst and competitive edge in leadership honed my skills and was refined by my twenty-one and a half years as an Air Force chaplain lieutenant colonel. I used that skill set to develop my core leaders. That core leadership development proved invaluable in the storm. The gravitational pull of the core leaders holds the church together.

"Weather Alert." The momentum of success in ministry can create blind spots that prevent us from seeing the warning and watch announcements that severe storms are headed our way. I share how I felt and what I did when people jumped ship in the middle of a multimillion-dollar construction project. The intricacies of a construction project are many and foreign to new leaders. I learned how to build a church and congregation at the same time. This took a lot of courage and consecration.

"In the Storm" unveils the chaos of all the things that can and will go wrong when banks do not fulfill their written commitments and your integrity is called into question. Cash management is essential in ministry. How to have enough cash to do ministry and build a multimillion-dollar building is not for the faint of heart, especially when you are in the midst of a storm. Creating community is difficult in the decentralized online world in which we live, and it is even more difficult when the wind from the storm is blowing so hard you are not sure if you are hearing "Hosanna!" or "Crucify him!"

"After the Storm." Bad times don't last forever. Getting through the tough times requires professional help. The torment and toll on one's soul demands counseling. Counseling brings about clarity of thought. This section is about the unsurpassing wins God brought me and my church to. It details the hard-fought victories, favor, and miracles wrought by the faithfulness of God.

PART 1

BEFORE THE STORM

1

CALLING

HOW WE GOT HERE

*Calling always matches who you are. . . . Nothing in life
is as rewarding as fulfilling your calling—nothing.*

JOHN MAXWELL

OLD GLORY FLAPPED IN THE WIND as congratulations rang from the crowd. I saluted smartly for the last time and walked off the stage of a successful military ministry career as an Air Force chaplain lieutenant colonel retired. The applause grew louder and louder with each passing month as I stepped onto another ministry stage, this time as a civilian church planter. Before long the applause from the rapidly growing church plant was so loud I couldn't hear the oncoming windstorm that would soon become a firestorm.

The executive pastor resigned and started his own church. The worship pastor quit. The youth pastor resigned and started a home Bible study. But that was just the wind. As in the days of Elijah, the earthquake and fire were around the corner with no still quiet voice to be heard. It was the firestorm of the bank twice reneging on its loan commitment. The multimillion-dollar construction project was stopped with the red iron beams of the sanctuary still suspended in the air. The explosive growth of the church imploded, and parishioners left as fast as they had come, resulting in an extremely tight church budget. On top of that, I was looking for a cave to go hide my life-threatening depression and anxiety so I could hear God's voice like Elijah. But there was no cave.

What kind of calling from God can give you the leadership skills to lead yourself and your core leadership team out of a situation like this? What do you do when you are nothing more than a shell of the sharp chaplain lieutenant colonel who once saluted smartly and is now struggling to hear God's voice while Elijah's words reverberate in your soul: "I have had enough"? When Elijah said this, he sat under a broom tree following a tremendous victory over Jezebel and Ahab at Mount Carmel.

> Then the fire of the LORD fell and consumed the burnt offering and the wood and the stones and the dust, and licked up the water that was in the trench. And when all the people saw it, they fell on their faces and said, "The LORD, he is God; the LORD, he is God." (1 Kings 18:38-39 ESV)

Despite the victory Elijah said, "I am the only one of the LORD's prophets left" (v. 22). He ran in fear of his life and battled severe anxiety and depression. He couldn't bring himself to attempt suicide, so he chose death by God, "But he himself went a day's journey into the wilderness and came and sat down under a broom tree. And he asked that he might die, saying, 'It is enough; now, O LORD, take away my life, for I am no better than my fathers'" (1 Kings 19:4 ESV). What kind of calling equips you for the moments in ministry when your mental health has had enough? A calling similar to that of Elijah—a calling that answers fully within one's humanity.

Elijah was a human being just like us (James 5:17). Sure, he called down fire from heaven and rode into heaven on a chariot of fire, but even he succumbed to the storms of ministry leadership. There are times when the isolation and demands of ministry can wear the strongest person down. A broom tree awaits every leader who dares to answer the call on their life to be used by God to the point that God empties them out. It is in those moments they must find a cave to go to, heavenly food to eat, and an acuity to hear God's voice in the midst of their pain.

Only when leadership skills move from theory to praxis can you hope to navigate the storms leadership will inevitably bring. My definition of a leader is someone with the ability to inspire people beyond their natural capabilities to accomplish a common goal or vision.[1] To execute one's leadership, you must withstand hurricane-level wind gusts.

You must also prioritize your mental health against the pressure to succeed and the pressure to serve. Elijah found a cave, but leaders are often unable to find a cave to go hear God's voice of consolation, strength, and direction. Additionally, many are reluctant to even admit they need a cave. The pressure to do God's will at all costs is immense. According to the Schaeffer Institute, 70 percent of pastors constantly fight depression, and 71 percent are burned out. Eighty percent of pastors say ministry has negatively impacted their family, and 70 percent say they don't have a close friend.[2] The data shows that it's not okay to say you're not okay when you are leading others in the body of Christ.

The heartache of leadership affects more than pastors. It affects anyone who stands in front of someone and asks them to do anything. The parking lot attendant directing parishioners to park. The usher at the door showing people where they can sit. The minister who will deliver the sermon. Leaders include business owners and parents who work in the home. Lifeway research shows that ministry leaders in all positions are negatively impacted—from personality skirmishes to squall lines of ministry, including full-blown hurricanes of denominational politics and church splits.³

No one is immune from the storms of leadership and the brokenness the storms leave in their wake. Church hurt is real, and many no longer volunteer or leave organized religion altogether.⁴ The number of ministry leaders considering quitting as of March 2022 is 42 percent, up 13 percent from January 2021. They cite the tremendous stress of the job, isolation, current political divide, the affects the job has on the family, and their lack of optimism about the future.⁵ What may be a simple drizzle of rain to one leader may feel like a life-altering gully washer to another.

Everyone experiences ministry leadership differently. Who would have thought the simple words of Jezebel would cause Elijah to have a mental and emotional breakdown?

> Ahab told Jezebel all that Elijah had done, and how he had killed all the prophets with the sword. Then Jezebel sent a messenger to Elijah, saying, "So may the gods do to me and more also, if I do not make your life as the life of one of them by this time tomorrow." Then he was afraid, and he arose and ran for his life and came to Beersheba, which belongs to Judah, and left his servant there. (1 Kings 19:1-3 ESV)

The Bible is good at bringing its readers behind the scenes to see, feel, and vicariously experience what the bigger-than-life biblical characters were going through. Too often, we read about their lives through rose-colored glasses because we already know the end of their story. When we pause and slowly read about their lives through the lens of their moment in context, we have a greater appreciation for the storms they came out of. Paul's shipwrecks are more real when we are floating in the water with him until he gets to the dry land. We can feel the snake bite when we know the island was slithering with snakes. And we can run from Jezebel like Elijah when we go behind the scenes with him.

THE EMPOWERMENT OF A BACKSTORY

It's behind the scenes when you see the test of ministry. When things are not going well is precisely when leadership is needed. The Bible is littered with the backstory of victory being wrestled from the jaws of defeat. The timber of a leader is seen during the winter storms that will assuredly come your way. When I was in the military, we called these storms backstories or lessons learned. Leadership would always want to go over those lessons learned immediately after war games. We called those briefings "hotwash." The need to discuss the good, the bad, and the ugly so soon after the war games was so that leadership could get to the backstory, which is where the learning took place and to understand what not to do next time.

So it is in ministry leadership. Behind every battle story of success is a backstory more breathtaking than the headlines. Leadership has its Mount Carmel moments. Leadership has its ten plagues, Red Sea miracles, daily manna, quail from heaven, water from a rock, and Jordan River crossing moments. It also has golden calf moments. The rewards and fulfillment of leading others to a closer walk with God and the manifestation of God's work in the earth are the lifeblood of ministry.

But the highs of ministry leadership can only be matched by its lows. Elijah had multiple ups and downs and even had to live within the famine he prophetically proclaimed: when the brook dried up, he had to eat from a dirty bird. Even Jesus was up one day and down the next: "You are my Son, whom I love; with you I am well pleased, " was followed by Jesus being driven into the desert wilderness by the Holy Spirit to be tempted by the devil. Luke makes sure we know that Jesus' victory was short lived. "When the devil had finished all this tempting, he left him until an opportune time" (Luke 4:13).

That was not all of Jesus' un-equilibrium with respect to his leadership development. In one moment, Jesus was self-assured and confident when John the Baptist sent his disciples to ask whether Jesus was the Messiah, "And Jesus answered them, 'Go and tell John what you hear and see: the blind receive their sight and the lame walk, lepers are cleansed and the deaf hear, and the dead are raised up, and the poor have good news preached to them'" (Matthew 11:4-5 ESV). In many ways Jesus "flexed" on his cousin John the Baptist by citing his accomplishments.

But in another moment, Jesus seemed less self-assured when he asked Peter and his disciples what was the word on the street about him:

> Now when Jesus came into the district of Caesarea Philippi, he asked his disciples, "Who do people say that the Son of Man is?" And they said, "Some say John the Baptist, others say Elijah, and others Jeremiah or one of the prophets." He said to them, "But who do you say that I am?" (Matthew 16:13-15 ESV)

In his infinite wisdom, God has permitted us the record of the Holy Writ to leave us these leadership backstories of highs and lows of Jesus, Elijah, and others for a reason. If they had their ups and downs, victories and defeats, times of popularity and unpopularity, so will we.

MY BACKSTORY: TALK OF THE TOWN

As Elijah was the popular leader of the school of prophets, I was the very popular leader of New Life Church, which led to me pastoring one of the leading churches in the community. Its rapid growth made New Life the talk of the town. From barber shops to hair salons, gyms to the mall food court, seemingly everybody was talking about this chaplain on Scott Air Force Base, Illinois, who had retired and started a church in a hotel ballroom. More than 850 people showed up for the launch service. More than 250 joined on the first Sunday, and the membership quickly grew to more than 2,000. There were so many people, we had to ask the brand-new hotel to give us more chairs as the ballroom was overflowing.

For a while it seemed like I had a Midas touch. Every ministry initiative I touched turned to gold. Souls were saved, lives were changed, and more LifeChangers (as we call ourselves) joined the church. Our ministry success drew the ire of many, but at the same time the highest form of flattery is when others begin to imitate your ministry model. My influence and that of the church grew rapidly like the corn in the fields all around us in our Midwestern community.

We started receiving awards for our work in the community along with grants for community initiatives. I was asked to serve on the local school board, the first African American to do so, as well as many of the boards that were recognizing our work. Civic leaders came calling for our support and endorsement even though we refrain from letting politicians speak to the congregation. We started a chapter of the NAACP and openly pushed being a racially diverse church. Our capacity seemed limitless.

This was not the first time my ministry seemed to have limitless capacity. At the tender age of thirteen, I preached my first sermon. Pentecostal United Holy Church in Goldsboro, North Carolina, was packed. There was no room for any more chairs, not even standing room. I heard the voice of God at the age of twelve when I gave my life to Christ. I was with a group of newly saved kids under an oak tree at the Southern District headquarters of my denomination. While debating the Scriptures, I distinctly heard God say, "Do you see how they listen to you? Lead them!" So, I told my pastor what I heard, and he scheduled my "trial sermon."

People had come from what seemed like every corner of eastern North Carolina to hear what an eighth grader would say about living holy. I mounted the pulpit with an overconfident air that only a young teenager could have, ignorant of the call on my life and what lay ahead. I read my text with the bravery of David going to fight Goliath.

Then Jesus was led by the Spirit into the wilderness to be tempted by the devil. After fasting forty days and forty nights, he was hungry. The tempter came to him and said, "If you are the Son of God, tell these stones to become bread." Jesus answered, "It is written: 'Man shall not live on bread alone, but on every word that comes from the mouth of God.'" (Matthew 4:1-4)

I announced my sermon topic like I was John the Baptist in the wilderness. With fire in my belly, I preached like Paul and said, "What you want is down here (I gestured to the floor like it was hell). What you need is up here (I gestured to the ceiling like it was heaven)." The announcement of the text and topic alone brought the house down with a thunderous "Hallelujah!" "Amen!" "Preach, boy, preach!" The moment felt like it was over before it started, a blur lost in the euphoria of accolades, and just like that my leadership journey was off to a roaring start.

My calling started early in life and gained steam every year as I actively pursued opportunities to lead whether as co-captain of a high school basketball team with a 24-1 record, becoming president of the Black Student Union, being voted one of the outstanding seniors of my graduating class of the University of North Carolina at Greensboro, or wearing the cloth of my country for over twenty-one years. The Air Force took my desires to lead and developed me into a sharp, self-assured chaplain lieutenant colonel. I hungrily devoured anything that smelled like leadership development—the continuing education of squadron officer school, academic instructor school, air command and staff college, the Air Force Institute of Technology special assignment, the many Air Force chaplain school short courses, the three master's degrees, and one doctoral degree

After the military I continued to learn more about leadership by earning my PhD in organizational leadership and being mentored by some of the foremost leaders in the body of Christ, including my spiritual mentor, my church consultant, Dr. Sam Chand, and my executive coach, Bishop Walter Scott Thomas. I became even more of a sponge, trying to absorb as much knowledge as I possibly could by going to every leadership conference I could find. Twenty-one-and-a-half years of the military culture of intense leadership, more formal education, an ever-deepening devotion to God, and commitment to the call on my life prepared me for the storms I would face, so I thought.

The military inculcated me into a world of routine, excellence, planning, and carrying out strict orders, and my call molded me. When I retired, I conducted myself in military fashion to plant New Life Church like Joshua's Israelite brigade when they marched around the walls of Jericho (Joshua 6:1-27). The church plant was a regiment of routine success in almost everything we attempted to do. Launching the successful church had me planning and executing like in Nehemiah 4:6-15. "So we rebuilt the wall till all of it reached half its height, for the people worked with all their heart" (Nehemiah 4:6).

It took us a little longer than fifty days to build the church. With the winds of success filling our sails, in eighteen months we went from having church services in a hotel ballroom to marching into the first phase of a multimillion-dollar church with a sanctuary, classrooms, administrative offices, gym, and preschool. The building went up so quick, people couldn't believe it. Nothing like that had ever been done in this community before. "Who is this preacher? How did they do it?" was the constant refrain. Doing my best to lead like Joshua, Elijah, Nehemiah, and Jesus was paying dividends. I also led like David—with heart, transparency, creativity, and youthful vigor. "And David shepherded them with integrity of heart; with skillful hands he led them" (Psalm 78:72). But none of that could help me lead through the gathering storms and life challenges I was about to face.

LEADERSHIP PRINCIPLES AND LESSONS LEARNED

The leadership theory that best reflects chapter one is authentic leader, which is characterized by the interpersonal, intrapersonal, and developmental leader.[6] The leader is reflective within and responsive without and strives to grow through self-discovery and applying those evolving developments to leading their followers. In growing and developing my calling to lead, I discovered areas that desperately needed attention and areas that were intuitive and innate to my personality and being. I used both to become a better leader.

A leader must be brutally honest. The transparency of the leader starts with oneself, and that authentic self-awareness can transform you into the leader God needs when the moment arrives. Take self-evaluation inventories, learn your values by doing values exercises, and journal (see the Appendix for recommended self-assessments). Habakkuk said write the vision and make it plain; I say write your story and make it plain. Find yourself so you can be yourself. People follow authentic leaders.

QUESTIONS FOR REFLECTION AND DISCUSSION

1. As you reflect on your calling, what are some of the milestones in your journey that prepared you for leadership?
2. List at least five challenges you are facing right now.
3. Have you ever felt overwhelmed by the demands of leadership? What did you do in response?
4. What are some of your coping skills?

2

CORE

THE STRENGTH OF YOUR LEADERS

*Your core values are the deeply held beliefs that
authentically describe your soul.*

JOHN MAXWELL

MINISTRY STORMS CAN BE LIKE the solar storms Captain Kirk of *Star Trek* had to navigate on the Enterprise. Early in my preaching career, I often spent Saturday evenings glued to the TV for another episode of *Star Trek*. Instead of reviewing my Sunday school lesson, I was being drawn in as Captain Kirk, Mr. Sulu, Mr. Spock, Lieutenant Uhura, Bones, and Scotty went flying through space at warp speed. Week after week, Captain Kirk and his core team encountered both the awesome beauty and great danger of the solar system. I had no idea back then that spending my Saturday nights with Kirk and his crew instead of my Sunday school lesson would help frame my understanding of leadership development in ministry. When I became senior pastor at New Life Church, I had to develop a core team that would help me navigate the turbulence of my ministry solar system the same way Kirk's team supported him. I realized that the core of my leaders was like the core of the solar system.

THE POWER OF THE CORE

The ability of the core is not only required to keep the solar system in place but also to determine its seasons. A core keeps a church in place and also determines its seasons. The first thing Jesus did was pray, then he picked his core (Matthew 10:1-4). Jesus knew crowds would come and go. Jesus knew that crowds wanted fish sandwiches and miracles, but it would be the core who would carry out the work of his ministry. John 6 gives us insight into how Jesus viewed his core and the crowd. Jesus knew the difference between the two—who would stay and who would go. Jesus didn't feed the five thousand to get them to stay nor did he feed them to follow him. Jesus fed them based on their need. He was not trying to have a crowd; his focus was the core. He poured himself into his core because he knew his earthly ministry and the subsequent ministry of the church would orbit it. When the crowd ate and ran, Jesus wanted to know what his core would do. The magnetism of that comes from the density of the core, which was Jesus' preoccupation.

> From this time many of his disciples turned back and no longer followed him. "You do not want to leave too, do you?" Jesus asked the Twelve. (John 6:66-67)

Jesus knew crowds were needed because crowds attract even more crowds and increase one's influence in the community. But a core is what turns the world upside down (Acts 17:6). However, Jesus' core consisted of twelve disciples whose imperfections were his constant concern and recipients of his individual attention. They bickered and argued about things like who was the greatest.

> A dispute also arose among them, as to which of them was to be regarded as the greatest. And he said to them, "The kings of the Gentiles exercise lordship over them, and those in authority over them are called benefactors. But not so with you.

Rather, let the greatest among you become as the youngest, and the leader as one who serves." (Luke 22:24-26 ESV)

To increase their gravitational pull, Jesus explained to them privately what it meant to use their influence as leaders.

Jesus was meticulous in picking his core followers because he knew they would be the leaders who would grow the ministry. The core would be the glue that others stick to during the formative developmental years of the church. They would have to shoulder the burden when the storms of persecution would put the early church under tremendous pressure. So, picking twelve imperfect people was no small undertaking. The core would either hold the solar system of soul saving together, or there would be a collision of leadership that could collapse the church Jesus purchased with his own blood.

When I planted New Life Church I, too, prayed and picked my core. The constant jostling for position was no different than it was for Jesus. I remember once it had gotten to a point that I asked my spiritual mentor at the time, what I should do. He told me that I was called to start a church, not a nursery for babies. He was referring to their immature actions. His advice was insightful but not strategic. So, I didn't immediately address the strategic issue of developing the core leaders who would hold the church in orbit during a storm. I later received counsel from Dr. Sam Chand, who gave me meaningful strategic advice, which I will discuss later in the chapter. Both advisers were helpful, but neither could foresee the storm that would crack this core.

CORE CRACKING

The business of cracks in the core began when my executive pastor and I had a sharp disagreement, not unlike that of Paul and Barnabas over John Mark's participation in planting churches (Acts 15:36-39).

After I decided to part ways because of our disagreement, I was never content with my decision, which was inconsistent with my nature to work through disagreements. I also had to deal with my letdown and total disappointment with our inability to reconcile our differences, because I cared deeply about him and saw him developing into a loving and caring pastor. I sought counsel as to how to handle this major problem, given that my initial decision didn't give me peace of mind. I asked a trusted colleague to give me advice, an old military friend who also knew my executive pastor. Additionally, I reached out to Dr. Sam Chand for advice. My old military friend gave me his take on our contention—make it public. However, Dr. Chand said making public our disagreement was an option, but it all depended on the culture I was trying to create and how much influence the executive pastor had within the church. In other words, would public acknowledgment of our disagreement hurt or help the church? I chose the advice of my trusted friend from the military. To this day I regret taking his advice.

Following my friend's advice started tremors in the core. Those tremors produced events that eventually fractured the core, resulting in an earthquake that shook the entire congregation. The church didn't split, but it surely splintered. An annoying but painful splinter underneath your fingernail or just beneath your skin can make life miserable. Our splintering was a problem that would affect our growth, leaving us searching for direction and needing time to overcome. New Life survived the splinter, but the damage had been done. Moreover, it created other fissures and cracks in the core that some core leaders saw as an opportunity to cause more splinters.

EARTHQUAKES OR TREMORS

When I moved to the Midwest, I experienced my first real earthquake. It wasn't the movement of the earth that woke me, but the noise the quake caused. It was like the roar of a lion with iron teeth and a deep rumble. It was disconcerting and frightening. Similarly, it was not the tremors and splinters of other key leaders leaving within months of my executive pastor starting his own church that did the damage, but the community narrative that the church was splitting and dying. Within months of the executive pastor leaving, my youth pastor and worship pastor left. They both had their reasons. Both said it had nothing to do with the noise, tremors, and splinters in the church made by others leaving, but one wonders. The worship pastor wanted to relocate back to Dallas, Texas, and the youth pastor took a government civil service job in tech. Both reasons were insufficient to quiet the storm at New Life. It felt like the rush of people jumping off the Titanic.

Keeping my leadership footing was ever more treacherous. The most difficult thing about an earthquake is that the earth beneath you is not stable. Nothing can anchor you. When your core is unstable, so is your church. Convincing people to stay on board a shaky foundation when they come to church for stability is a losing proposition. The last thing you do is make it worse by announcing the departures from the pulpit on a Sunday morning.

Yet that's exactly what I did. I had not yet learned from my previous pronouncements about construction delays that simply communicating bad news was not the thing to do. I have this obsession with honesty and transparency. I didn't want people to ask where these leaders had gone. I didn't want those who left to control the narrative, so I was determined to explain the situation to the congregation. I would thank them for their service and not get into the minutiae, but what I learned is that whether you say it, people create stories you can't control.

Years later, I attended a retreat at my spiritual mentor's house where he said, "Never give your enemy the microphone." He was watering sons in the ministry with a water hose of wisdom. He told us about the many attacks he had dealt with. He said that responding to negativity elevates it and gives it a voice it would never have had if you said nothing. Responding to blogs, tweets, and posts only increases the social media engagements. Therefore, don't give them your mic.

Oh, how I had needed that advice sooner! I had elevated their departures to Sunday morning status. What a huge mistake. I should have handled it as a simple staff change. At the most, I could have let our vision board know. People leave jobs all the time. People make career choices all the time. Why were these treated differently? Let me stress this point: leaders will face transition. Transition must be handled correctly, with wisdom and discernment. Timing is everything. Sunday morning is the wrong time to tell the congregation anything bad. There is no time to answer hard questions. They didn't come to hear bad news about you or the church. They came to be uplifted and connected to Jesus Christ. My desire for transparency should not have dictated the timing of my announcing the challenges of the church.

During our church tremors and fissures, the church was indeed shaking, but it didn't crumble. Why didn't it? With the core being cracked and significant leaders and staff leaving, what was the glue that was holding everything together? Even though some people left New Life, those remaining in the core still had tremendous gravitational pull.

REGRETS AND 20/20 HINDSIGHT

When your world is shaking you will almost automatically latch onto the familiar. In the throes of the leadership upheavals, I reached out and grabbed ahold of a friendly familiar voice. My longtime military friend had good intentions and his advice was based in a scriptural reference: "But if any of the leaders should keep on sinning, they must be corrected in front of the whole group, as a warning to everyone else" (1 Timothy 5:20 CEV). But context is important, and the whole counsel of God is critical. Scripture also says restore a person when that person is found in a fault: "Brothers and sisters, if someone is caught in a sin, you who live by the Spirit should restore that person gently. But watch yourselves, or you also may be tempted" (Galatians 6:1).

Based on my context and church culture of grace and forgiveness, I should have applied the latter text and not the former. Everything in me told me to do that, but listening to the familiar in a crisis, I made the wrong decision. Had I followed the essence of how God created me, I believe the outcome would have been different. My nature is to forgive. My tendency is to overlook an offense.

This miscalculation made me revisit who I seek counsel from. Moreover, it revealed a valuable truth: professional counsel is far better in a crisis. The professional advice of Dr. Chand had years of experience and a breadth of similar situations to draw from. His counsel was also objective. The counsel from the old military friend was misplaced because he was also a friend of my executive pastor. That lack of objectivity should have been enough for me to go the other way.

Hindsight is 20/20. Paul said we see through a mirror dimly; we see in part, so we know in part (1 Corinthians 13:12). Therefore, we do in part rather than in perfection. The ramifications of leadership decisions have a lasting impact. They can determine the growth trajectory of a church and the direction of people's lives. Leadership decisions rarely have the luxury of what in my military days we called a "do-over." Leaders must walk by faith and not by sight. Leaders pray hard and make the best decisions they can in the moment. Then God works it together for his good. God takes our decisions and factors them into his will so that his will on earth is carried out. There are at least three factors that I believe God used to ensure the vision of New Life Church was carried out.

Factor 1. When I first started the church, I did not meet with the core leaders regularly. The press of a new church plant and building a multimillion-dollar building at the same time took all my attention. Over time I realized the many fires I was putting out that emerged from my core leaders was a direct result of my disconnection from them. So, I started monthly leadership forums in which I would teach a lesson on leadership. This connection enabled me to be proactive in my leadership. It increased relational connection between my core leaders and myself. It gave them access to me, so they could be heard and contribute. This increased the density—the relational unity and strength—of our core. Density increase causes the gravitational pull of a planet to multiply. The reason the sun can hold so many planets in orbit is because of its density, which is 12.4 times that of Earth.[1] Even though it had some cracks, New Life Church held together because our core was densely constructed.

Factor 2. The remaining core did not like the way the others left. While the crowd did not care to know the facts and relished in the innuendo, rumors, and palace intrigue, the core knew the real deal. They knew I had acted in good faith. Even though I had made mistakes, they knew my heart was in the right place and my motives were not to cause anyone harm. They also knew the individuals who left. I have come to realize that the leaders of a church, or any organization, have conversations to which the senior leader will never be privy. They had their own opinions about those who left, and those opinions only intensified their commitment to the church.

Factor 3. The third factor was vision. The leaders who remained were committed to the vision of the church. The proverbial writer said it best, "When there is no prophetic vision the people cast off restraint" (Proverbs 29:18 NET). Vision has the power and gravitational pull to keep the church on track. The remaining core wanted to see the vision through. They refused to get distracted. The vision became a rallying cry.

During my twenty-one and a half years of military service, I learned the importance of a rally cry. In the fog of war there must be a word or phrase that those who are embattled will reconnect with and reconstitute their resources. The battlefield can be a confusing, chaotic place, so before the fight, as part of the war plans, a word or place is decided upon that calls everyone to assemble when the enemy is taking ground. I have seen this work during training for battle. Now I have seen it work in a real spiritual battle.

Our rally cry in the battle was, "To change more lives for Christ." This caused the core to rally, reconstitute, and reconvene what we believed God had started in us. The church started with strong vision casting, and it was that factor that kept the moment from becoming personal offenses that further divided us. Vision kept us orbiting the Son.

LESSONS LEARNED

It is next to impossible to lead without learning how to lead better. Capturing the lessons learned is critical to becoming a better leader. John Maxwell says leaders don't fail, they "fall forward." Here are the following ways I learned to fall forward.

First, I learned how to pick a core. Often leaders trust their instincts in picking who will be a part of their core leadership team. Our instincts can be spot on many times, but other times they are completely wrong in discerning character, spiritual maturity, loyalty to the vision, integrity, and acuity for leading. Jesus offers an example that I added to my tool belt for picking leaders. Jesus prayed before picking the Twelve (Luke 6:12-16), he chose a diverse group of disciples, and, most importantly, he picked people who had been "picked over." One could argue they were rejects. During biblical times, mothers would bring their children to the rabbi in hopes he would pick their sons to be his disciples. Jesus alludes to this when mothers brought their children to Jesus and he says, "Suffer little children, and forbid them not, to come unto me: for of such is the kingdom of heaven" (Matthew 19:14 KJV). The twelve disciples were men who were never picked. Rejects!

After praying all night, Jesus picked them out of the hundreds following him, including some of John the Baptist's disciples. Twelve men who had been "picked over" and who had found other occupations to fulfill their purpose. From Judas to Peter, Jesus selected diversity and inclusion. Being picked after being looked over can generate an internal tenacity for followership and belonging within a person.

Additionally, in ministry you must pick who God sends, not who you hope God will send. Jesus developed the disciples into leaders who would turn the world upside down (Acts 17:6), and you too must develop leaders. I prayed and picked a diverse group of leaders. Some faithfully served well, a small number not so much—just like Jesus' leaders. But the core held New Life together.

Second, a God-given vision will not inoculate you from leadership fissures, but it will keep your church or organization from crumbling when the earth beneath your feet violently shakes. A godly vision is what brought New Life into existence. There was no ego of wanting to be the senior pastor of a large church. There was no ambition to satisfy. The gravitational pull of an assignment to do God's work in the earth is critical. Every organization, family, and individual will have challenges, but what will hold things together is a biblically grounded vision from God.

Third, I learned you have to engage leadership development consistently for your leaders. The more they hear your voice, the better they will follow. Create your own lesson plans that connect to the church or organization's vision. At New Life, we have a theme for the year that reinforces the church's overall vision. To reinforce the success of the theme, my leadership lesson plans are connected to it. During challenging times, it will not seem like a five-alarm fire if you are already meeting regularly. There will be no need to call an emergency meeting to put the fire out. You will also be able to establish the fundamentals of leadership that will permeate the culture of the church.

Fourth, build up yourself and your core leadership. Like David, encourage yourself in the Lord (1 Samuel 30:6). Most exercise routines involve your core. The stronger your core, the more weight you can lift. It is also the area that is prone to be flabby and reflect bad eating habits. The core leadership must have a regular, nutritious, balanced diet of leadership development and spiritual development along with biblical knowledge. This diet must be supplemented with regular reminders of the vision.

Finally, the untimely departure of key leaders gave me expertise akin to the leadership theory called Leader-Member Exchange (LMX), which has to do with the leader forging meaningful relationships with the in-group (core group) and the out-group (not a part of the core group) that exists in every organization.[2] Those in the in-group are the closest to the leader and produce more. They do this based on their relationship capital gained by having access to the leader. They readily go above and beyond for the leader and for the cause/vision of the organization. The out-group, not so much. They put their time in and go home. They expend enough energy to meet the stated goals and needs of the organization but no more. They aren't as close to the leader and are not as bought in to the cause/vision of the organization.

Core

The leader must be careful to balance the needs of the organization with the real needs of these two groups. The degree to which the leader is successful in achieving this balance will match the level of success in accomplishing the vision of the organization. Leaders who easily transition out of your core can be identified as those in the out-group. Their allegiance is to their own agenda as well as a transactional relationship. These types of leaders need not be punished for their out-group behavior and desire to transition.[3] One must recognize this early in the relationship and not hold them so close to your heart. They are not in-group leaders.

Leaders who are in the in-group number should be afforded grace, especially if grace is a value and cultural ethos you are trying to grow in the church. I made a huge mistake by not giving my executive pastor grace. He was an in-group leader and had earned it by his loyalty. He was not a clock puncher. LMX theory and Scripture supported grace, but I listened to well-meaning, inexperienced counsel. Dr. Chand said it best, "What type of church are you trying to develop?" Lessons learned can be painful.

This theory, in a practical sense, is like the core and crowd of a church. Both have needs. Both require attention. Both must trust the leader. Both have worth. A crowd attracts a crowd, and a core holds things together. An example of this is seen in Jesus' interactions with Peter, James, and John—the in-group/core—and the nine out-group/crowd. Jesus led both by giving special attention to Peter, James, and John by taking them to Jairus's house to heal Jairus's daughter; the Mount of Transfiguration; and the Garden of Gethsemane. They got special attention. He gave the crowd fish sandwiches and was okay when a percentage left (John 6).

While I would later write my dissertation on LMX, I had no idea God was giving me a crash course beforehand. I led both groups, even though some got fish sandwiches and left based on their own agendas. The core stayed intact.

QUESTIONS FOR REFLECTION AND DISCUSSION

1. What development programming are you using to strengthen your core?
2. What Scriptures and leadership principles do you teach your leaders? How often do you offer this instruction?
3. What are some practical ways you are building relationships with those who are disenchanted with the vision and part of the out-group?
4. What leadership principles and theories are you applying to your core, yourself, and the out-group?

PART 2

WEATHER ALERT

3

CONSECRATED COURAGE

PREPARE FOR THE STORM

What makes the dawn come up like thunder? Courage.

The Cowardly Lion in *The Wizard of Oz*

Forecasting the weather isn't new. Jesus said as much in Matthew 16:3, "And in the morning, 'Today it will be stormy, for the sky is red and overcast.' You know how to interpret the appearance of the sky, but you cannot interpret the signs of the times." When we interpret the sky that says our weather forecast is bad, we prepare accordingly. The worse the forecast, the more we prepare. Depending on where you live, you may be familiar with the weather patterns and know how to prepare as soon as the forecast is announced. I live in an area of the Midwest often referred to as "Tornado Alley." We are always on guard for tornado forecasts.

One day my son and I were out for some bonding time. We had breakfast at a restaurant and were wondering what to do next. Should we go to the mall or go home and watch a movie? We had no idea that our minds would be made up for us. We are East Coast born and raised, which is why we were unaware of the forecast that day. We weren't even in the mindset that a few cumulus clouds could turn into a tornado. As with many tornadoes, a hailstorm preceded the tornado. Tree limbs and hail flew by the windshield as I drove as fast as I could to get us home and into the basement. The car was battered along with the roof and siding on our house. We made it, but just barely.

Tornadoes require you to shelter in a basement or closet to get away from flying debris. Hurricanes can cause flash floods that require you to seek higher ground. Preparation for snow or winter storms requires you to make sure you have fuel or heat along with enough food and a generator in case the power goes out. But how do you prepare when you don't even see the storm clouds gathering—when you don't see the signs of your times? Not only did I not see the storm approaching, but I also confused the thunderous applause I heard as I stepped off the stage of a wonderfully successful military chaplain ministry career with the rumble of thunder in an Elijah-type thunderstorm. Preparation is key to surviving the storms of life and will help you get through life. But when a cataclysmic storm catches you off guard, what helps you to survive?

I was not prepared for the multiple storms that came my way soon after I planted New Life: key staff abruptly resigning, church growth slowing down, and the banks not keeping their word. The voice of the late James Cleveland comes to mind: "The tempest would rage, and the billows would roll."[1] Given that storms in life are inevitable, there are some things we can do to prepare, even when we don't know they are coming—when we don't know the signs of our times.

ATSO

While I was serving in the military we had to learn wartime survival skills. They were called "the ability to survive and operate," ATSO for short. When I planted New Life Church all I could see were the promises of God coming to fruition. Like Joshua, who took the million and a half children of Israel across the Jordan River and into the Promised Land, I was taking my church into the promised land of winning souls and changing lives.

Joshua was one of the two spies that had a minority opinion about whether the newly freed Israelites could defeat the enemy and possess the land. He spoke up strong and early, along with Caleb, but both lost the vote. Later, he got a second bite of the apple to lead. Unlike my first church plant, which began with a handful of people while I was on active duty, this time there were hundreds of people who joined on the first Sunday we had public worship service. It reminded me of what a colonel told me during a one-on-one leadership mentoring session: "The larger the command, the more opportunity for things to go wrong." So it was with Joshua and me.

With his feet on the banks of the Jordan, Joshua had no idea what he was about to step into. His command was a million and a half people who didn't know what wilderness life was and who had no warfare skills to fight for the Promised Land. What was Joshua's pedigree to do what God had called him to do? How did he end up in this position to lead God's people? Joshua was the son of Nun (Numbers 13:8, 16), a soldier's soldier in the battles in the wilderness (Exodus 17:9), and the servant, protégé, and disciple of Moses.

Joshua was very much like the attaché of the general officers I saw when I was in the military. They were always by the side of the generals, carrying their briefcase, like when Joshua went with Moses up to the mountain of God and saw the tablets in Moses' hands (Exodus 32:15-20). Once I met the attaché of the president, as he carried the "football" with the nuclear codes. He never left the president's side, and I never met a sharper officer. I can only imagine Joshua was equally as attentive to Moses (Exodus 24:13).

Few leaders are as fortunate as Joshua to be a part of a divinely orchestrated succession plan. Few are fortunate enough to have a Moses as a mentor. Church planters are essentially successors of themselves. They are the first pastor and there is no discussion of someone coming after them. God is their heavenly mentor, and they often have to convince people God has his hands on them as he did with Joshua and Moses. Convincing people to follow in a storm was no easy task for Joshua, but he was mentored by the best. Moses did what God told him to do concerning sharing his authority. God told Moses to deputize Joshua by bringing him in front of the people and laying hands on him. This rich tradition of laying hands on one's protégé was a sign to everyone that Joshua was the God-ordained successor (Numbers 27:18-23). Someone once said there is no success without a successful successor and Moses followed God's orders to the letter to ensure success.

Joshua, with the power of God at his back, miracles of ten plagues, morning manna and afternoon quail, miraculous snake healings and water from a rock—I believe Joshua with his toes in the banks of Jordan River could have possibly had a range of emotions in that moment, too fearful to go forward because he felt unprepared for the forecast. Even though Joshua had reason to be courageous—"Now Joshua son of Nun was filled with the spirit of wisdom because Moses had laid his hands on him. So the Israelites listened to him and did what the LORD had commanded Moses" (Deuteronomy 34:9)—he was still afraid, and he felt unprepared. God still had to tell him not to be afraid. "Have I not commanded you? Be strong and courageous. Do not be afraid; do not be discouraged, for the LORD your God will be with you wherever you go" (Joshua 1:9). I believe God had to tell Joshua not to be afraid because he did not know what was in front of him and he felt unprepared for what was in front of him. The only way he could lead was to consecrate himself to prepare himself for the unknown; he had to develop the ability to survive and operate no matter the challenges he faced.

I found comfort and instructions for my life through the lens of Joshua's life and how he learned ATSO. Joshua reminds me a lot of myself. He had bouts of doubt when he should have been filled with faith. So did I! He lacked confidence when he should have been courageous. So did I! There were times when he felt his responsibilities were bigger than him, but he rose above all that by a devoted life of prayer and consecration. So did I! Like Joshua, I found strength and courage in consecrating myself and those around me. Prayer and my first book, *Prayer Answers Guaranteed*, became my staff to steady me. Like Joshua, I leveled up my ability to survive and operate as best I could for the storms, but even in all that I was far from perfection.

CONSECRATION

Poised on the shores of the promises of God, Joshua convened his leaders and prepared for the wilderness and promised land of leadership. He made a declaration that turned his fear into faith and his suspicions into stable steps of leadership. "Consecrate yourselves, for tomorrow the Lord will do amazing things among you" (Joshua 3:5). Consecration is a confluence of a period of prayer, fasting, devotion, journaling, quiet time, and more—all this and then some are what I did when I stood at the precipice of God's promises and planted New Life, even though I did not know what was ahead. I did what my mother told me when I was a boy preaching to adults with no idea of the hell in the lives they faced. She would say, "Son, you will preach before thousands, so you need to consecrate yourself."

Hearing her voice in my head in the beginning of the church plant, just before I saluted and marched off the stage of my military career, I obeyed the Holy Spirit and went on a four-day consecration. Days before my retirement ceremony, I locked myself up in a cheap hotel room with a case of water and my Bible. I prayed, read my Bible, journaled, and slept. I thought I was doing that for the promises I was about to step into. I did not know it was for the storms I was about to go through.

Like with Joshua, the promises were before me, and the fear of the future made me cautious. I knew from my being a preacher's kid there would be challenges. I saw my dad double down in his determination. He was an intense, passionate man who raised eleven children, pastored two rural churches, and tried his hand at entrepreneurship. Whether it was family problems or church problems, with limited resources he was steady, consistent, and determined. I was the apple that didn't fall too far from the tree. But even with preparation, how do you know if the times you are in are a cataclysmic multi-storm that will last for years? How do you prepare yourself and your leaders for that? Joshua has some more insights.

MILITARY DISCIPLINE FORMATION

First and foremost, Joshua was a military man who found his confidence in order, structure, and routine. We had that in common. Without knowing what was ahead, I emulated Joshua's life in many ways. When he came to the unknowns, he sent spies to do a reconnaissance mission. When I planted the church on my retirement, I had what the military called an ADVON team, which was like a reconnaissance team. It was a select group of leaders who did all the legal paperwork to establish the church plant. I could not have anything to do with the legal formation of the church to avoid any conflict of interest of me potentially persuading military members to leave the chapel services and start a church.

When Joshua stepped into the Jordan it was with precision. The priests had their position. The people had their position. The cadence of the march had to be precise, and everybody had to fall in line. Military discipline is critical when you are confronted by an enemy you know little to nothing about. Sun Tzu says the art of war is to "know your enemy, know yourself."[2] Suffice to say, when you don't know your enemy, your future, or the storms you are about to face, know yourself even more. Self-leadership, being self-aware, and having self-reflection as you move into a new church plant is critical.

Joshua led a million and a half people who were neither versed in wilderness trials nor spiritually mature. This meant in addition to knowing himself in order to defeat an enemy, he had to develop leaders to fight the pending battles. Leadership development was no small undertaking for Joshua. Not only did he have to develop their military fighting skills, he also had to develop them spiritually. Circumcision was a public deterrence for the men of Israel to be identified if they went to a house of ill-repute. Circumcision was also public leadership preparation via pain (Joshua 5:7-8). Leadership development requires self-discipline, cutting off the extras of life that prevent fulfilling the fullness of the call to lead on one's life—a kind of circumcision.

It is hard to prepare people who have never been circumcised by life or fought together. Stepping into promises they lacked life experience for took courage and consecration. As my mother used to tell me when I was a boy preacher, "Son, it's more than a notion." Our Jericho was going to be building the people and the church building at the same time with the forecast of storms the weatherman didn't tell us about. More about those storms later.

Israel crossed the Jordan and came to the first storm, the heavily fortified city of Jericho. Jericho was also the firstfruit of the promise. Its walls were so thick and wide that chariots could crisscross as they patrolled. Joshua set up a military formation and game plan to confront their first storm. The only thing that brought down the fortified walls of Jericho was military precision, ATSO, and consecration. The wisdom of God is hidden from the ways of men (1 Corinthians 1:25), but the wisdom of God produces outcomes because the walls of Jericho fell and the Israelites marched in (Joshua 6:15-17).

We mistakenly see this story as a miracle without military meaning or organization. In other words, we think this miracle is not rooted in the warfare of the day. Noise was part of the ammunition of warfare. Gideon used it: "The three companies blew their horns and shattered their jars" (Judges 7:20 BSB). Goliath used it: "Goliath stood and shouted a taunt across to the Israelites" (1 Samuel 17:8 NLT). Here Joshua was using the arsenal of regimented order—military precision. God ordained noise to bring down the walls.

Even though I was not aware of storms ahead, the fervor of our worship, praise, and prayer life, helped prepare us. People gathered from all around the metro to join in with the joyful noise of the new church plant. I didn't know these were preparatory steps for foreboding storms. They were a part of my theological foundation for starting a church. Military precision produced Israel's victory when the walls of Jericho fell. Worship, praise, and fervent consecrated prayer prepared me for the storms we had no clue were coming our way. Like Joshua had his own storms to get through, I too faced internal struggles that threatened to sink our ship. They were a part of the unseen turbulence ahead.

THE DEVOTED THINGS AND DIVISION

The storms within are as difficult to discern as the signs of your times, and often the applause, cheers, and celebration of a victory over a storm can dull your spiritual senses. So it was with Joshua. The victory over Jericho was the shot in the arm his leadership needed. The region was clearly abuzz about the Israelites coming as

Rahab testified, "I know that the LORD has given you the land, and that the fear of you has fallen upon us, and that all the inhabitants of the land melt away before you" (Joshua 2:9 ESV).

Jericho, the fiercely fortified city, fell to the consolidated noise of praise, and victory was still in the air, but so was disobedience and division within the ranks. Because Jericho was the first city to fall to the hands of Israel it was kind of a firstfruit. God always gets the first of the harvest. It doesn't matter what it is. Beginning with Cain and Abel there is a long biblical history of God wanting the firstfruits of what we have. It was not that Cain gave a grain offering and Abel gave the best of his flock. Cain did not bring God the first portion of the harvest (Genesis 4:1-5). When we trust God with the first of what we have, there is no guarantee we will get a second harvest or flock. Therefore, giving God the first is a tremendous act of faith.

Jericho was a type of firstfruit, and the bounty from the city (silver, gold vessels, bronze, etc.) was supposed to be devoted to the Lord. Joshua did his best to develop his leaders, but Achan must have slipped through the cracks and took some of the bounty for himself. He hid it. His actions cost the Israelites an easy victory. They were defeated hands down at Ai (Joshua 6:18-21). They missed the obvious when it came to Jericho being devoted to God, a fatal error that caused division within Joshua's "church plant." Now their future victories were overshadowed by the storms of internal division.

God's promises were real and permanent. No matter the storms that raged, they could not erase what God had for Joshua's leadership. Joshua could not have predicted a few would have their own agendas that could affect the many. What does Joshua's story have to do with preparations for the storms that arose during me planting New Life? It required Joshua and the rest of the Israelites to consecrate themselves again. They consecrated themselves when they were about to cross the Jordan and they had to consecrate themselves again following Achan's disobedience. Planting New Life required constant prayer, fasting, and consecration.

When they prayed, the who and what of the problem was revealed. The consecration cracked the community code. Joshua had to start with levels of leadership within the "new church plant" from tribes to families to clans to get to the culprit within. The consecration created the critical criteria by which the problem was revealed and resolved. This leadership skill was repeated as Israel prepared to seize the promises of God and plant the new million-and-a-half-member church in the Promised Land. Joshua's lessons learned were invaluable for me going forward. The self-development of consecrating oneself through prayer, fasting, journaling, devotion, and quiet time with self-reflection sharpens the leader's skill set to lead.

LESSONS LEARNED

I remember attending a ministers' conference at the outset of planting the church after my retirement. The sermons and lectures were all about strategies to get through the storms of ministry. I thought to myself, *Life couldn't be better*. The church was growing by leaps and bounds, and all seemed well with my soul.

Battles are inevitable. Preparation is intentional. As I went to the lectures and listened to the encouraging sermons, it occurred to me that perhaps this was a time of preparation for storms I could not see coming. The sermons and seminars addressed the various problems pastors faced. I remember someone saying you're either coming out of a storm or going into a storm. It was neither for me. It was all sunshine and blue skies, but a quiet voice kept telling me, "Your storm season is going to come. These men and women in this conference are trying to tell you something." They had all been beaten down by the ministry and were warning those of us who have yet to experience their woes to get ready.

Serve the Lord so you can be prepared with whatever he permits to come your way. Prayer, consecration, purposeful praise, and a devoted lifestyle are intentional preparation for unavoidable storms. Jesus said it best in his parable about the house. If you prepared yourself and built it well, it will withstand the rain, rising water, and blowing wind. If you did not, it will fall (Mathew 7:24-28).

Jesus had just finished delivering the Sermon on the Mount when he spoke this parable. He had reclassified Scripture and updated the laws. Then he told his listeners the parable that gave them word pictures of the outcomes. Applying his teachings would prepare them for the inevitable, unrelenting storms to come. When my mother used to tell me to turn my plate down and pray and make that a part of my life, it proved to be a critical part of my life's preparation for storms. She would say to me, "Son, remember God is still on the throne, and you need to pray and stay prayed up." That was her way of saying no matter what comes your way it will never exceed God's power to help you overcome it and get you through it.

Prayer became and remained a pivotal part of my spiritual formation, so much so that I wrote my first book on the topic, *Prayer Answers Guaranteed*. When I was a PhD candidate, I was surprised that one of the comprehensive exam questions was to elaborate on spiritual formation. In my worry as to whether I answered the question correctly, when I got home, I went through all my books on that subject and found this highlighted quote, "Central spiritual practices indicated by New Testament authors include worship and prayer."[3] The book was a used textbook. I did not highlight that line with the volumes of reading I had to do. But clearly consecration and prayer are key ingredients in preparation for doing the work of God, as evidenced by the previous readers of the textbook.

When starting a church or any venture for God, the victories will come, but don't become intoxicated with success. Doing so will dull your spiritual senses of discernment. At best we "know in part" (1 Corinthians 13:9) and can never see all the storm clouds gathering around the corner. Therefore, spiritual depth is anchored in the harbor of a consecrated and devoted lifestyle. No biblical character escaped the storms of life. All too often, we read about their victories and fail to see the wisdom of God's intentionality in leaving their mistakes, missteps, sin, and storms as lessons learned. Not everyone will comply with the culture of the community. Like Achan and his crew, some will cause storms and exacerbate the inevitability of storms.

LEADERSHIP PRINCIPLE

Situational leadership best describes Joshua's approach to leading Israel into the Promised Land after the death of Moses. Situational leadership is when the leader adapts their style to the context, situation, and competencies of their followship. The situational leader is directive and supportive with their followers to achieve the goals of the organization. The situational leader, as its name implies, assesses the situation and determines how to best accomplish the vision despite the roadblocks. If the followers are self-motivated and high capacity, the situational leader is not as directive.[4] In the case of the defeat at Ai, Joshua learned his followers were not as competent or motivated to do the right thing as he thought. He changed approach and took a more directive approach to deal with the reality and the possibilities for future battles.

In preparation to plant New Life, my leadership style adapted to the conditions on the ground. The forever changing dynamics of leading a church requires flexibility and adaptability, two terms that are frequently used in the military. The Air Force says flexibility is the key to air power. The army says adapt and overcome. Both phrases have to do with warfare. When a fighter pilot is in air-to-air combat, the pilot must learn how to trust their instinctive flexible instincts to win the battle. In the army, ground forces encounter unforeseen terrain and enemy obstacles that they had not planned for, but they adapt to the situation and overcome to be victorious. The situations confronting the leader are always changing and what worked last week will not work this week. You cannot preach the same sermon week after week and neither can you use the same leadership skills for every problem you encounter.

QUESTIONS FOR REFLECTION AND DISCUSSION

1. How do you prepare for life's storms? How do you prepare those you lead through storms?
2. What is your first response to life's storms? What is fueling this response?
3. Which biblical character do you identify with when you are in life's storms?

4

CONSTRUCTION

HOW TO BUILD THE CHURCH

The people had a mind to work.

NEHEMIAH 4:6 ESV

THERE IS A DIFFERENCE BETWEEN building a church building and building the people in the church. The apostle Paul said, "Don't you know that you yourselves are God's temple and that God's Spirit dwells in your midst?" (1 Corinthians 3:16). To build either one is a massive undertaking. Building both people and temple at the same time is tantamount to having an affinity for stress, pain, and pressure. When you walk off the stage of a successful military career and into a church plant where 850 people show up for your launch service, you feel compelled to build people and a building at the same time. A lot of people followed me from the worship service I led at Scott Air Force Base to see what all the fuss was about. Only days after the launch service, I announced during a Sunday morning worship that we would build the church building in eighteen months.

As we launched, I had signed an eighteen-month contract for the use of the hotel ballroom where we held our services. I told the hotel manager we wouldn't need it after then. With no loan from a bank in hand, I wouldn't have made that audacious statement to build a doghouse let alone a church house. But with the same vigor and overconfidence in faith I had on the night of my initial sermon, I spoke the words God put in my mouth: "We will build the church building in eighteen months." I received the same outburst of amens and hallelujahs as I got when I preached my initial sermon.

Just as I stepped off the military ministry stage to applause ringing in my ears and into an oncoming storm that would drown out the claps, so it was with trying to build a church building and church people at the same time. The phases of building a church building were something neither the military nor any of the schools I attended taught me. Loan applications. Vetting architects. Vetting construction companies. Understanding the phases of construction. Blueprints. Environmental studies. City ordinances. Building permits. City council approvals. Planning and zoning. First reading. Second reading. Public hearing. Opposition. Construction phase. Change orders. Price increases. Material selecting. Value engineering. Construction complete. Walkthrough.

It is all so stressful, especially when your frame of reference is limited. It is even more stressful when you are simultaneously leading people in a new church plant. And did I say I didn't even have a loan to build when I told the church we would be in a building in eighteen months? Yes, I have an affinity for pressure. Many believe that a person does better under pressure and while multitasking, but research finds that is simply not true.[1] The stress and pressure to perform can cause emotional and physical pain, even strokes and heart attacks. I am thankful that the tremendous pressure didn't "break the pipe." Though there were times when it came close.

The weight of trying to build a church building and build people most certainly brought me to my knees. I felt like I was Jesus in the Garden of Gethsemane, but unlike Jesus, I had no fellow ministers to fall asleep while I prayed. I was in the winepress of church building and growing church people by myself. This was my inexperience in leadership. I had not yet developed relationships with my spiritual mentor, Dr. Sam Chand, Bishop Walter Scott Thomas, and others. I kept to myself, which made things even more difficult for me, and at times I had a deep feeling of being alone. Some of my colleagues in the area looked at me with suspicion rather than give me collegial support and friendship. The best I could do at times was to prioritize the two competing challenges and fall back on two things—the discipline a twenty-one-and-a-half-year lifestyle in the military injected in me and my father's example.

CRASH COURSE

When I said we would build a church in eighteen months I did so with my father's experience in mind. He led a congregation that celebrated reaching a Sunday morning offering of $250. It was situated between railroad tracks, a trailer court, a junkyard, and a muddy field at the end of a dirt road. The rural family church leadership was quite content because this space had become sacred, jam-packed with people at its twice-a-month worship services. My father had a vision to move the church to higher ground—literally. The crawl space underneath the building was always flooded and the bathrooms might as well have been attached porta-potties. With fierce opposition, my father won the motion to build a new church by a whopping one vote. Half the church minus one opposed building. It was his tenacity, faith, and confidence I observed and emulated in building both church and church people. Watching him was my crash course in building a church building.

My crash course in building the people in the church occurred while I was a chaplain in the Air Force, six years before I retired. It was a joy to pastor the congregants that attended the worship service I was responsible for. I woke up every morning looking forward to what the day would bring as a chaplain pastoring active-duty members of the military. Pastoring well-disciplined, focused, highly educated Air Force personnel is not the same as pastoring a church plant. Yes, it had its challenges, but they were minuscule compared to growing a civilian church plant.

Given my love for people and penchant for pastoral leadership, while in a chaplain headquarters staff position in Washington, DC, my boss permitted me to plant my first church. That was highly unusual, but he saw that while I was good with the paper side of ministry, my heart was with the people side of ministry. Not only did he approve of me planting a church while on active duty, he approved the Air Force tuition assistance for me to earn my Doctor of Ministry degree in church planting.

In short order, I was a doctoral student taking a crash course in growing a civilian congregation and planting a church while serving as a full-time chaplain staff officer in Washington, DC. I planted the church in Hampton, Virginia, and went to school in Richmond. Every week for two and a half years, to quench my thirst for pastoral ministry, I drove seventy-seven miles from northern Virginia to Richmond, and 165 miles from northern Virginia to Hampton on Sundays. The sacrifice was great, and the learning scholastically and pastorally intense. My studies were highly informative educationally but didn't prepare me to build a church building and the church people at the same time six years later. Planting the church in Hampton, Virginia, certainly did. It showed me how not to plant with respect to inadequate resources and more zeal than wisdom. Boy, did I learn my lesson.

NO LOAN

I was and continue to be the quintessential walk-by-faith-and-not-by-sight kind of guy (2 Corinthians 5:7). I believe in calling those things that are not as though they were (Romans 4:17) and that if you decree a thing it will be (Job 22:28). I quickly learned that God's word needs to be accompanied by more than just your faith. His word needs to agree with his will in the moment of a plan, a people, and the prayerful faith of others. Additionally, it needs to be accompanied by a vision from God. In the moment of my declaration, I was not aware that the Illinois bedroom suburbs area of St. Louis needed the very type of church God had laid on my heart to plant.

God assembled a core group of people—mostly active-duty and retired military—who were willing to be guarantors of a multi-million-dollar loan because they believed in the vision God had given me. My declarations and bodacious faith statements were not me whistling in the gale winds of construction. God gathered men and women from around the world to be the sail that grabbed the vision wind and went to the bank with me. We had in hand the assets of 11.5 acres of land that a single donor helped us buy. The late Deanne Rayford heard me preach a sermon on tithing where I asked, "Who would give $100,000?" No one raised their hand. I said, "Then no one wants to be a millionaire, because $100,000 is the tithe of $1 million." I did not know Deanne would give $100,000 and more and that she had been praying about what to do with a large sum of money she had received. After just two applications we were approved. All of this happened in an amazing short period of time, unlike the loan to expand the sanctuary.

As with Jesus, the core must include some men or women with business acumen. Many of the disciples were in the fishing business. If possible, try to have some on your core team with a successful business background. A diverse team is critical.

We had a strict requirement that all core leaders pay tithes and give sacrificially to the capital campaign. I learned the value of the core leaders' gravitational pull, which caused others to see and support the vision. Now I was managing a multimillion-dollar construction project when my only experience in money management was a $1.5 million budget acquisition I managed while on staff six years earlier and watching my father build a family-size church in my early twenties. But my inexperience was mitigated by the core management team. Building the building was fraught with problems, but the collective faith and expertise of the team brought the project to an expected and declared eighteen-month completion. This was matched by my systematically building the people.

BUILDING CHURCH PEOPLE IN A CHURCH PLANT

I quickly learned that zeal and a love to pastor people are not enough to plant and grow a church. Vision, systems, structure, intense evangelism, discipleship, and a model that works are what it takes to plant and grow the people in the church. So, I set out to develop the vision, systems, and structure. I started with plenty of research and by answering a line of questioning one of my professors asked, "What do you think God is up to in your context? What's your hypothesis for how to build people and grow a new church plant?" I came up with five concepts I believed would grow the people in a new church plant.[2]

Teach the core group a progressive approach to evangelism. When I say "progressive," I am talking about evangelism that considers the way the church appealed to and propagated the gospel message a generation ago and modifies it to fit into a fast-pace, "want-it-yesterday" society that has two basic concerns: time and safety. Our progressive approach is quick and safe for the individual who is evangelizing and considers the anxiety people feel about being approached by strangers.

Teach the core group and each new member the principles of the church. Today, core values are taught in the business, government, military, and the private sectors for good reason. When individuals are taught the basic beliefs of an organization, they become grounded in what the organization deems important, and they aspire to carry it out. The church is no different. This is especially needed for a nondenominational church. Therefore, this new church plant has a set of principles (called the seven Ps) that are the impetus for ministry and are the broad boundaries by which New Life Church (NLC) does ministry:

Progressive: NLC believes God is not static but relates to his people within the context (time and place) of their life situation.

Proclamation: Luke 4:18—NLC believes the gospel/Word is essential and central for salvation.

Preparation: 2 Timothy 2:15—NLC believes Christian education in all forms (Bible school, Sunday school, parochial education, etc.) is vital for Christian maturation.

Prayer: 1 Thessalonians 5:17—NLC believes continuous communication with God is essential for the church to hear God's will for the church.

Praise: Psalm 150:5—NLC believes in a vibrant worship experience that is under the leadership of the Holy Spirit, which allows all other aspects of worship (Scripture reading, singing, prayer, proclamation, etc.) to meet the holistic needs of the congregation.

Perspective: Genesis 10:1—NLC believes identifying, discovering, and being affirmed by the multiracial Scripture is an absolute must to understand how we are made in the image of God.

Prosperity: 3 John 2—NLC believes in economic development and overcoming systematic poverty, oppression, and political apathy as a part of holistic living, along with eating a diet that is conducive for healthy living.

Define the target group and evangelize them using our progressive approach. In some cases, terms like *target group* are shunned because they seem market-oriented and not "spiritual" enough for a church. In fact, the notion of "whosoever will let them come" is still very prevalent in today's church. But there is a growing sense that this approach of going after everyone is not working. It is in that vein I believe God will enable this church to grow. I believe if the church clearly identifies who we believe God has called us to minister to and evangelize them, then the church will grow.

Teach a comprehensive new member's class and systematically assimilate new members into the church. So often new members are left to find their own way in their new church home. They are not told the expectations of the church and may never get integrated into areas of the church that use their God-given gifts. The basic tenet of Protestantism is the priesthood of every believer. That belief will be fully activated by the comprehensive new member's class. When that doesn't happen, some new members get discouraged and disillusioned. Growth for a church comes from people who are assimilated.

Teach the vision to every member. People without a vision soon perish (Proverbs 29:18). Another translation says without a vision, people run wild. If there is a vision from God given to the pastor and taught to the core group, the church will be destined to grow. The vision also distinguishes the church as an arm of God. It is important for those who are establishing a church to recognize they are not starting a business, though some solid business principles are needed. Neither are they starting a social club, though social interaction is important for the climate of the church. They must understand they are starting something God has ordained.

The church is the place where God dwells, and reconciliation for humankind is carried out by way of a God-centered vision. Many churches believe the pastor is to do the ministry—preach, teach, visit the sick, pray, bury, marry, and never miss a potluck. The pastor is to equip the body of Christ to do all those things and more, but principally, the pastor is to equip the people to do the ministry (Ephesians 4:11-12). So I curated a culture that empowered members to see themselves as LifeChangers. Therefore, leaders must create systems, framework, and structure to equip believers. I decided early on that New Life would develop leaders because a disciple of Christ is a leader. Jesus said to go rise your influence to make more Christ followers (Matthew 28:19).

Central to building church people was my fixation on developing leaders. I developed our leadership model by creating monthly leadership classes and annual leadership summits. That evolved into iLead Academy, with online courses through a learning management system. Plus, every leader in the church was required to attend monthly leadership development forums, which had basic spiritual formation sessions. As the leader goes from one level of leadership to the next, they take our online leadership development courses that conclude with an encouragement quiz to move the person from one lesson to the next.

THEORETICAL LEADERSHIP MODEL

New Life Church's leadership model is steeped in understanding leadership in a broader context and the church context. Leadership is the bent and culture of the church. Leadership has global reach as one of the most researched disciplines in academia due to its impact on an organization.[3] It is the topic of discussion from sports to politics to government to business to the military and the church. Given that it is needed for the success of an organization, one would think successful church models would abound other than the traditional models from the Eurocentric milieu. That has proven not to be the case.

Exercising leadership is complex and depends largely on the organization, the followers, and the leader's circumstances. The model I developed at New Life to build the church building and church people was born out of necessity, using the model I developed for my DMin project. The approach of implementing my project hypothesis gave me a framework, and the experience of implementing that model during my first church plant while on active duty equipped me with the theological and biblical basis to plant New Life in Christ. It was God's grace that both church plants experienced a measure of success. This praxis approach also helped me develop and fine tune my definition of leadership.

MY DEFINITION OF LEADERSHIP

In developing the theoretical and biblical foundation for growing church people and building a church building, defining leadership is critical. Although there are many definitions of leadership, I have come to define it as this: the ability to inspire people, beyond their natural capabilities, to accomplish a common goal/vision greater than themselves. How do you do this? By creating dissonance and a need or desire to change. You must cast a vision that causes dissatisfaction with the status quo or the present condition. Ask yourself why people should change and follow you into that change.

To inspire people is God-oriented. It is not manipulation or coercion. Ask yourself why people follow you. Is it because they are paid to do so? Because they can't find a better job? Is it because they believe it is their duty? Or do they see the activity of God in your life? Do they sense that God is with you? Do you have a track record of success? Inspired leadership is based on the work of the Holy Spirit. You will not have to prove God is leading you. His presence will be self-evident in the fruit produced in your life. The common goal or vision is always what God wants done in the earth. People come together to experience and achieve something they cannot achieve or do on their own—to be a part of something greater than themselves. We hunger for such as God has designed us to work together to do his will. Leaders enable this process to unfold. It is truly the Lord's work. We have an innate desire to leave our mark—from the graffiti artist to the gang member who spray paints their colors and signs to the lovers in the park who carve their names in the bark of a tree.[4]

LEADER LESSONS LEARNED

As I discussed in chapter two, leadership development of the core will make or break your church. I learned that leadership development needed to be biblically and theoretically based. It needed to be consistent, efficient, and applicable. Building the building and building the people at the same time was unavoidable for me. A new church plant should focus on first building people who would in turn build the building. I do not advise doing both at the same time.

You may have heard the African Proverb, "If you want to go fast, go alone. If you want to go far, go together." This idea that working with others is more effective and productive than working alone is taught in Scripture. Ecclesiastes 4:9 says, "Two are better than one, because they have a good return for their labor." Many others echo this message on the importance of teams. Entrepreneur and venture capitalist Reid Hoffman once said, "No matter how brilliant your mind or strategy, if you're playing a solo game, you'll always lose out to a team."[5] Basketball legend, Michael Jordan explains, "Talent wins games, but teamwork and intelligence win championships."[6]

We teach leaders that teamwork is more effective than working alone. So why don't we naturally gravitate toward teams? Why do we need to be intentional with team-building efforts? Because healthy, productive teams require time, energy, and intentional leadership. The late basketball coach Pat Summitt once said, "To me, teamwork is a lot like being part of a family. It comes with obligations, entanglements, headaches, and quarrels. But the rewards are worth the cost."[7] Team building requires building trust, handling conflict, setting goals, empowering vision, and managing diversity.

There are several different types of teams. There are temporary teams like short-term mission teams or project teams. High-capacity teams include groups like a church ministry staff or an organizational team. Teams can be functional, typically in the same department or organization, working on related tasks. They can also be cross-functional, including individuals with diverse experiences or from different departments or organizations. In some cases, teams are led in a top-down hierarchical manner with a leader directing the team's activities. More commonly today, we are seeing the power of self-managed or high-autonomy teams in which the leader empowers and encourages the team to make decisions, solve problems, and collaborate toward the team's goals. New Life Church incorporates all the above to develop our leaders.

QUESTIONS FOR REFLECTION AND DISCUSSION

1. Do you hold regular leadership development classes, seminars, or workshops?
2. If you do, what is the focus of the development?
3. Is leadership development a requirement for all leaders in your church or organization? Why or why not?
4. Do you regularly seek out information or opportunities to develop your leadership. If yes, how often? If no, why not?

5

CANCELED

WHEN PEOPLE JUMP SHIP

We must accept finite disappointment but never lose infinite hope.

MARTIN LUTHER KING JR.

ON DICTIONARY.COM, according to the pop culture section, *cancel culture* refers to

> the popular practice of withdrawing support for (canceling) public figures and companies after they have done or said something considered objectionable or offensive. Cancel culture is generally discussed as being performed on social media in the form of group shaming.[1]

New Life had not done anything objectionable or offensive to be canceled by the culture, but to me, it felt like we were being canceled when people started jumping ship. Sheep scatter easily. When they get disturbed, they unwittingly leave the flock in search of peace. When New Life faced storms of key leadership leaving, the construction project stopping, red iron beams standing with no roof, and banks reneging on their word, a lot of sheep canceled me and the church. It wasn't so much because of what we did as what we didn't do or couldn't control. Jesus couldn't make all his disciples stay either (John 6) and no one can make a bank keep its word. Those details mean nothing when sheep decide to "cancel" you and leave for other flocks.

In every cancellation, God is working out his plan. Nothing that happens in a believer's life gets past the hands of God using it for the good of building his kingdom and accomplishing his will on earth. God also uses it to develop the character of the believer (Romans 8:28). The Bible is full of biblical cancellations, some of which were orchestrated by God and others used by him to develop his leaders. Enter Gideon.

Today's society would love to think it invented this popular cultural practice of canceling someone, but as Solomon said, "There is nothing new under the sun" (Ecclesiastes 1:9). In 1209 BC, Jerub-Baal (most of the time we call him Gideon) was canceled long before cancel culture existed. His fellow warriors carried out the act as he prepared to fight the battle of his life for the life of his people. God called Gideon to save Israel from the hands of the Midianites (Judges 6:14). The task was daunting, and Gideon had his doubts he could do it (Judges 6:15). After a considerable amount of time and testing by God, Gideon accepted this enormous call on his life, but that is when the story gets interesting.

Jerub-Baal, which means "Let Baal contend," had his forces cut. Gideon was losing supporters in droves. The first cut came in Judges 7:3, "Now therefore proclaim in the ears of the people, saying, 'Whoever is fearful and trembling, let him return home and hurry away from Mount Gilead'" (ESV). Then twenty-two thousand of the people returned and ten thousand remained. His army of fighting men walked away in fear. Their reduction was drawn by God to ensure his glory, but the effects of God orchestrating this reduction of forces was a modern-day canceling of Gideon. But that was truly when the fun began.

Gideon went from thirty-two thousand to defeat the Midianites and do God's work to a mere three hundred. This was a 99 percent reduction. The job didn't get reduced to the number of men. The call was not rescinded by God. In fact, God doubled down and then gave Gideon an unadulterated plan to defeat an army that overwhelmingly outnumbered them (Judges 7:4-6, 9-10, 19-21). It was an open secret God was behind this cancellation. Some cancellations, whether cultural or spiritual, still have God's fingerprints all over them for his purpose will prevail.

When the momentum shifted to soldiers bailing, it seemed like it would not stop. One can argue Gideon's "cancellation" was different from that of the social media influencers, culture stars, and those who hold sway in our world today, but the outcome is the same. Followers will jump ship. One day you're up and the next day your followers have abandoned you. One day, I was up with more than enough soldiers to carry out God's call on my life and cause in the community. Then I got canceled.

The reasons are never the same and often you wonder if people are telling you the truth when they leave if they even talk to you upon their exit. All you know is being canceled for whatever reason doesn't feel good. You can never know why you get canceled. It begins to feel like the whole process is completely out of your control—because it is. New Life did not experience the reduction Gideon did, but our 15 percent reduction of LifeChangers had the same impact on me. It resulted in reduction in budget, volunteers, and momentum. Gideon's percentage was far more. Any season of reduction, desertion, or contention within the ranks when you are trying to plant a church and build a building is impactful.

While the culture cancels you—some within and others outside the church—your reputation is negatively impacted. Your influence is greatly diminished. Someone said, "All you have is your word." It takes a lifetime to build a reputation and a minute for the match of cancellation to set it ablaze (Proverbs 22:1; James 3:6). I felt the flames burn to my very core. Moreover, when the narrative about a church in the community goes from positive to "canceled" it impacts future growth as well as the church's current reality.

It's not just the narrative of the church, it is also the narrative of the leader, the senior pastor. The church has more time to overcome a cancellation, but a senior pastor only has a finite period of time to grow a church. The fruitful period of a senior pastor is not without a shelf life.[2] Therefore, while my cancellation was somewhat comparable to Gideon's given our aggregate numbers, the impact is relative. My tenure as senior pastor was at its pinnacle. I didn't have much time to surface on the other side of the cancellation. I would need God to add more years to my season of overcoming the growing narrative in the community, which I'll discuss further in chapter ten.

MANAGING THE BAILOUTS

While at first my duty station as a chaplain at Moody Air Force Base in Valdosta, Georgia, I remember being so proud of reaching my military career goal of being a chaplain. I had spent nine years on active duty in another career. When I met the educational requirement of a Master of Divinity, the Air Force changed my career to chaplaincy. This was my lifelong dream. Finally, I was a chaplain ready to serve both God and people. Every morning when I put my uniform on, I was beaming. My feet barely touched the ground when I walked. Shoes shined. Crisp uniform. Ready to serve the world, or at least the Air Force.

One day I walked into the Base Exchange (the military's version of Walmart) and the cashier asked me if I was the new chaplain.

Word had spread fast that not only was there a new chaplain on base but that he was also African American. I proudly said yes. She said, "You are either going to push 'em or pull 'em!" My face betrayed my failure at attempting to understand her southern accent, so she repeated herself, slower this time, "Chaplain, you are either going to push 'em or pull 'em. They're either going to come to your chapel service or they're going to leave your chapel service. You're either going to grow that chapel or it is going to dwindle down to nothing based on you."

By the time she finished, I didn't need an interpreter for her southern dialect. I got the message. I was either going to cause growth or cause an exodus. John Maxwell says it all depends on leadership. It rises and falls based on leadership. As I walked back to the chapel, I wasn't floating anymore. Reality was setting in. How do you manage the call of God on your life, the cause you believe he has given you to do, and deal with cancel vibes at the same time? No matter the situation, the moment must be managed.

After Joshua led the Israelite army in a miraculous victory at Jericho, he went into a battle against a less formidable file at Ai, but the Israelites lost the battle because Achan held on to some of the spoils from the victory at Jericho against God's command. Nonetheless, like Gideon, Joshua was able to secure a victory because of how he managed the moment. He called the entire leadership before him, started with tribe leaders, and worked his way all the way down to clans, then families, and then individuals. He uncovered the culprit of disobedience. Gideon "fleeced" God until Gideon's confidence grew to the point that he obeyed God as to how to reduce his number to God's glory size.

Everything depended on the leadership of Joshua, Gideon, and me. My bailout management consisted of several things:

1. I preached a sermon series on Joshua and Gideon. I held them up before LifeChangers as illustrative examples of what a church should do when people jump ship. I reminded them God permits things to happen in the life of the church to build its dependency on God.
2. I called the church to periods of prayer and fasting and consecration.
3. I captured the moment with encouragement quips that spoke to the moment.
4. "All we have to do is stay together" (see Genesis 11:6).
5. "God has called our church to do the hard thing."
6. "God was making sure we don't get full of ourselves and fail to give him the glory" (see Judges 7:2).
7. I preached a sermon on how to get through tough times called, "Ten Ways to Get Through Tough Times." For number ten, I told the story about my mother encouraging me during a difficult time when I was in the military. She said, "Son, I'm gonna call the prayer warriors to pray, but you remember this one thing: God is still on the throne." To this day, LifeChangers say, "Remember rule #10: God is still on the throne."
8. Make sure you don't hang around faithless friends.
9. Finally, I made the banks the foe. To motivate people, you must have an opponent that they are called to defeat.

Biblical characters' lives offer examples to make a point of your strategy to manage the storms that are certain to rise during your tenure of leadership. Take their leadership jams, contextualize them, and make them your own. In doing so you will embody said biblical characters and the principles of leadership.

THE WHY OF BEING CANCELED

Why were people not as committed as I had hoped? Why were people here today and at another church next week? Why do people say one thing and do another with respect to supporting the vision of the church? Why does cancellation manifest painful brokenhearted feelings as a senior pastor in feeling like a failure when you are being canceled? Gideon tells us why. "The Lord said to Gideon, 'You have too many men. I cannot deliver Midian into their hands, or Israel would boast against me, "My own strength has saved me"'" (Judges 7:2).

God insists on getting the glory when we carry out his assignment (Isaiah 42:8). He uses our situations to reduce the numbers to increase our dependence on him. Gideon was stressed by the reduction even though this was a part of Israel's warfare readiness to check and see who was ready for battle.

When God permits the community to cancel you, he is doing you a favor. God is weeding out the unproductive ones. Pruning is painful but it produces the fruit needed in battle (John 15:2). Struggles bring purification. God purifies your motives, your character, and your heart. God also uses the purification process to show others who you really are. It's what God did with Job whose struggles were never revealed to him. As the leading actor in this cosmic drama, you would think God would have let Job read the whole script, but he did not. Job had to learn his lines each day of his trials while his friends Eliphaz, Bildad, and Zophar ended up canceling him. Even when Job tried to inquire God's answer was insufficient to answer his anguish (Job 38:1-8).

Whether it's Gideon, Joshua, or Job, God always has a purpose behind being canceled. It may not always be self-evident. Experiencing people jumping ship in ministry is a part of ministry. To better understand the comings, goings, and canceling by church members you must look at motive.

THE GIDEON, JOSHUA, JOB EFFECT

Not many of us if any of us can compare to Gideon, Joshua, and Job. In fact, we can't compare to any of the characters in the Bible, but God ensured the biblical writers recorded their stories so we could see their humanity and God's divinity for our faith to digest in difficult times.

As Gideon's faith faltered, it was inconsistent. He didn't see himself as being up to the job. There were so many days where I felt the same. The stormy season made me question my decisions, second guess myself, and repeatedly ask God for confirmation. There were countless times when I found myself in bank boardrooms asking for a loan to complete the construction. I was full of fear and rejection, so I wrote Hebrews 13:5-6 on a piece of paper: "Keep your life free from love of money, and be content with what you have, for he has said, 'I will never leave you nor forsake you.' So we can confidently say, 'The Lord is my helper; I will not fear; what can man do to me?'" (ESV). I would repeat it to myself while explaining to new banks why the previous bank pulled out. I was doing self-talk while telling the story of the church. I felt like previous banks and people had wrongly canceled me, but I couldn't chase the misinformation of the cancellation.

I felt like Joshua as people abandoned me for their own motives and self-interests. I knew our Jericho victory of building a church in eighteen months would require maximum dedication from the moment I stood before the church in the hotel ballroom and declared that outrageously faithful statement. I never even considered some within the leadership ranks would say by their actions that one Jericho is enough. They had their own ministry goals and objectives in mind. While everyone has an individual call on their lives, it is my job to help all the sheep fulfill their individual callings. When they pursued their calls without notice, I felt betrayed. I felt like Judas had just come and laid a big ol' wet one on me and Peter was warming his hands by the campfire of denial of New Life's goals.

I felt like Job, as though God had put me on display to prove a point to the community that an African American man could build a major ministry in the conservative suburbs of St. Louis. As the season of struggle turned into years, my family support crumbled. My bride became tired of construction talk, bank talk, who-left-the-church talk, and updates on what people were saying about me behind my back and the church. There were times when I felt all alone with the words of Job's wife ringing in my ears, "Curse this construction and die." While those words were never said, it felt like it when my family grew tired of the toil of ministry.

The ministry of New Life is not even a minuscule of the ministry of Joshua, Gideon, and Job, but seeing their humanity and the enormity of their ministry helped me to see God's divinity and digest more faith to make it. I saw God's presence in how the consecration culture of Joshua, relentless obedience of Gideon, and stick-to-itiveness of Job ushered in enough moments of sustainment for me to be able to manage those elongated moments—literal years—of cancellation.

MEMBERSHIP MOTIVATION

While I was on active duty working on my Master of Divinity so that I could become a chaplain, I remember my church administration professor asked this question: "Why do people come to church?" Admittedly, I barely heard the question in between me nodding off. Being a full-time Air Force officer in a demanding career field was taking its toll. Driving from Langley Air Force Base in Hampton,

Virginia, to Richmond to spend the weekend in class all day was no picnic. When I came to, I remembered him writing all the reasons my classmates had given him: Looking for a mate. Business opportunity. Coerced by a spouse or love interest. Tradition. The reasons filled the board. At the bottom was salvation. I was shocked the professor did not dispute our random non-scientific findings. His point was the motives for church attendance are not always why pastors answer the call to ministry. That became self-evident when the storms hit, and people jumped ship. Their commitment to the vision of the church was not as deep as I had hoped.

The reasons why a person cancels you and your ministry may have nothing to do with you as with their motives. Gideon gives us great insight into why people jump ship—they never really had the same motives for going into battle. In Judges 6:28-32 we see an example of this. Many of the men in Gideon's army were motivated by self-preservation. They feared fighting the armies of Midianites. They were far more interested in canceling Gideon than standing up to the followers of Midian. Self-preservation is a strong motivation. When a church loses its new car smell because of storms, people don't want their reputations tarnished by attending "that" church with the problems. Leaders who have their own ministry aspirations also have self-preservation of ministry opportunity. So it was for many at New Life.

TERRITORIAL

While I was on his staff as the active-duty liaison officer, my boss used to tell me the military branches' internal fights always boiled down to power and territory. In order push his agenda forward in the highly political Pentagon, he would find out what the individual branches of the service wanted. He told me to find out the territory that is under dispute because that would determine how to resolve matters. When territorial matters are not adhered to, there will be canceling on one side or the other. This is also true in ministry. People will jump ship when they feel they are not gaining enough leadership territory, influence territory, high profile exposure territory, or proximity to the senior pastor territory. In a new church plant, all these territories have yet to be determined. The developmental stage of the church plant is still fluid. Jockeying for a position is common.

Jesus dealt with this in the formative stages of his ministry (Mark 10:39-40), and while he addressed this jockeying for territory, the issue persisted. Paul had to address it with the young Corinthian church when schisms and divisions rose among them (1 Corinthians 1:10-13). Territorialism within the church will cause people to cancel you. Unlike a social media cancellation when leaders and members cancel your leadership for whatever reason, it can have an impact on your ministry. When a church becomes the "go to" in the community, aspiring leaders see opportunities to lead at the highest and most popular level in the community. Their motives can cause conflict and territorialism. New Life was that church and the storms exposed territorialism motives.

LESSONS LEARNED

Because of the tremendous influx and rapid growth of New Life, being canceled did not sink our ship in the storms. Managing the momentum mitigated the long-term effects of people coming and going—a member of our church one Sunday and of another church the next.

I decided early on that when leaders left, I would not have them leave in the dark of night without explanation. I was very deliberate about convening a meeting of core leaders and explaining why they left. Preferably, when the exiting leaders complied, I would have them do it. When it came down to members of the church who were not leaders, I put them in demographic categories. In other words, if there was a consistent demographic group leaving such as young families, young adults, seniors, or single moms, I'd ask myself whether the trend points to something more than dispute over territorialism. If yes, our leadership team would try to address it programmatically. If no, then we had another way to try to find out why.

I learned that when people decide to leave the church, they prefer to keep their anonymity and simply stop showing up. This made for awkward moments with them at places like the mall or the grocery store. I remember shopping one day and seeing someone I recognized who was a member of the church—or so I thought. When I struck up a conversation with them in the food court, I spoke like they had been attending. Their child bluntly said, "Mommy, we don't go to that church anymore." They sheepishly admitted they were attending another church. We both had a nervous laugh and quickly ended the conversation.

Momentum can mask a lot of problems. It can also make many feel insecure about ministry, especially when people leave for no apparent reason. There was no storm when it happened to me. Just turnover, like employees at a big box store or fast-food restaurant. That insecurity will make you change your ministry to please who is no longer there to please. They voted with their feet.

The solution to this insecurity is a clear vision because frequent programmatic changes create an unstable culture if they continue, which will only exacerbate the problem of membership turnover. People come to church for stability. When the church is always changing its programming and discipleship ministries it communicates instability (James 1:8).

I soon learned to stop trying to figure out why people were coming and going and start focusing on those who were coming and staying. You can never stop people from leaving out the back door, but you can focus on the front door and why people stay. So, I began to ask people in new member's class why they joined. I developed surveys to ask volunteers and leaders why they stayed. The results were that the Word was taught in a way they could understand and apply to their lives, and that the children's and youth ministries were helping the young people. This information did four things: it affirmed the leaders, volunteers, and me; it took away the feeling of insecurity; it put gas in our tanks; and it gave us information to further strengthen our successful areas of ministry.

Managing when people jump ship can keep the momentum of the growth of the church. Momentum is everything in planting a church. It gives the church credibility that its product is worth trying in a crowded field. Like the new restaurant in town, the wait is worth it if the meal is managed and served well.

LEADERSHIP PRINCIPLES

When people jump ship or cancel you, that is a crisis. Whether you look at the crisis through the lens of Joshua, Gideon, Job, or Jesus, the leader must respond. Crises can cripple your church and even destroy it if you don't have a plan. I responded with a crisis management plan:

Acknowledge. You must recognize you are in a crisis. Ignoring the moment will not move it off the radar. Over spiritualizing the crisis as "the devil" will not make it go away (1 Peter 5:8). Satan is always on the attack but over spiritualizing the attack gives him more credit than he is due (Matthew 16:18). It can cause a "woe is me" victim mentality within yourself and the congregation and absolves you of responsibility to act.

Accept. You had a role to play in the crisis, whether you failed to do appropriate risk analysis of the church, made faulty decisions of faith, or simply made a mistake. Accepting your role is key to overcoming the crisis.

Assess. Determine how deep the damage is. Every crisis damages the church. Take a deep dive into the spiritual healing, attendance, giving, community narrative, and personal pain the crisis has brought on the church.

Aware. Devise a communication plan to share the crisis with all the stakeholders. How will you communicate? Text? Email? Small group? One on one? When will you communicate? Sunday morning? Over coffee or lunch? What will you say? Will the conversation be granular or high level? Will you blame and find fault or point stakeholders forward? Ask for input from stakeholders to devise a plan.

Arrive. You must arrive at a plan to move the church beyond the crisis and back to a place of stability. Take the input from the awareness step and use it to formulate a plan, though at this point you should already have a framework in place. Transformational leaders are always well-equipped for crisis response.[3]

Apply. Once you have a plan to move past the crisis and apply appropriate pressure on the wound so the crisis can coagulate, know that it may be a while before you can change the bandages or take them off completely. While crises are not chronic, they can last a while before the church can return to a sense of normalcy.

Alter. Be flexible and alter the crisis management plan of action if necessary. Flexibility and the ability to adapt and overcome is critical in crisis.

Allow. Finally, allow time for healing and recovery. Be patient with the process and constantly point the congregation to better days with an eye toward faith and an understanding of how crises are part of God's plan (Romans 8:28). God's plan will cultivate a culture of skills to build the kingdom and sustainability as with Joshua, Gideon, and Job.

QUESTIONS FOR REFLECTION AND DISCUSSION

1. Have you ever felt like you were canceled? If so, what did you do?
2. We all have love languages, according to Gary Chapman.[4] How do you articulate your feelings when you've been canceled?
3. What are the biblical characters you look to as examples of overcoming rejection?

PART 3

IN THE STORM

6

CHAOS

MULTIPLE THINGS CAN GO WRONG

All great changes are preceded by chaos.

DEEPAK CHOPRA

SAPAN SAXENA SAYS, "Every chaos has an order hidden in it. What we see as a chaos, is actually driven by a very disciplined and dedicated order of things. What we need to do is focus on the stuff before us, make our way through this chaos, and that order will sort itself out for us."[1] Believe it or not, there is a leadership theory called Chaos Theory.[2] While pursuing my PhD in organizational leadership I briefly ran across it in my studies and learned it well enough to cite it in one of my online dialogues to satisfy the discussion requirement. While I cannot remember the exact conversation, I do remember asking myself why anyone would come up with a theory that espouses chaos in any organization.

The ideal for an organization is order, which produces better outcomes. Little did I know that chaos was about to pay me and my church a visit and become an out-of-order member for the next few years. It leaped off the pages of the books and articles I was reading and right into my situation. The weight of PhD studies and the chaos I was experiencing at times was overwhelming. At other times it provided a convenient escape from the chaos and the demands of a fast-growing church.

A COLD DAY IN HELL

Since the congregation was growing, we needed more space. Our leadership had a vision for growth that entailed substantial expansion of our physical church footprint. It was a stretch to be sure, but my leaders and I believe in a big God who can make bold visions happen. As the founding and senior pastor of our church, I staked my ministry life on enacting this vision.

After months of a capital campaign to raise the necessary funds and multiple sermons on why we should expand our physical footprint with a larger sanctuary, more small group classrooms, and specialty community gathering spaces, it happened: we were finally building. Order was the order of the day, and we were bearing fruit everywhere until one bitterly cold Thursday morning.

I drove into the parking lot of the gym. As I was getting out of my car to face the subzero Midwestern winter, my phone rang. It was the banker who funded our church construction project. She told me she had her superiors in the room and that I was on speakerphone. Suddenly, the inside of my car felt colder than the weather outside. I had a sinking realization that something wasn't right. She wasn't friendly or engaging as in times past. She was straightforward and monotone. I froze in fear.

She told me straight away that the bank was no longer going to fund the project because our congregational giving was not what they wanted it to be. As such, they would no longer spend any more money on the project. I was confused, shocked, and hurt. In one phone call, my life went from the order of a routine morning to total chaos. I saw my ministry life flash before my eyes. We had just started. We had red iron framing in the air. The congregation was happy and thriving. How could this be happening? What did I do wrong? Why was the bank going back on their word? How would the congregation view me as their leader?

Three weeks before the call, the bank had sent us a notice following a site visit they conducted to check on the progress and discuss why the capital campaign was lagging in forecasted pledges. During the site visit we had an in-depth conversation about a new goal of raising approximately $800,000 in less than two months; we agreed to the demands. Now forty-five days from the agreement, by God's grace we were on track to raise the additional money and we only needed an additional two to three weeks to meet the amount in the new agreement.

The bank wrote the church a letter codifying the agreement with stipulations if we didn't raise the funds. After we had received the letter, our loan officer called to tell us to disregard it. She said it was "just a formality." So we did. We disregarded it, but that formality soon became a firm cease and desist for our construction project.

After the horrible call ended, I sat in my ice-cold car and called the church's chief financial offer. I told her to miss the scheduled staff breakfast and meet me so I could tell her about my heart-breaking conversation. I did my best to keep my voice from quivering, figuring that she needed to hear strength and resolve. I was literally shaking as I drove home. The only strength training I had that day was believing. "I will get through this morning," I told myself. When we met, I recounted the call in heart-aching detail. She was startled and deeply alarmed.

We called the bank back, demanding to talk with the loan officer and anyone else who participated in this betrayal of trust. The bank officials assembled. We put up a brave front as they listened, but then they told us to read the letter: "We are within our rights even though you are a couple of hundred thousand dollars from reaching the goal." From that moment and for the next few years, my life was turned upside down. I began living a version of the chaos leadership theory, not according to its definition but according to my reality.

How could a bank be so dishonest? How could they say one thing, write another thing, and then do neither? This isn't the first time banks have played a role in significantly impacting the institutions of African Americans and our communities. We find a long history of such in the United States.[3] From the redlining of Black neighborhoods and housing appraisal bias, which impacts property values, to foreclosing on Black churches at a higher rate than majority-led churches, African Americans are continually asked to play the same game while being presented with different rules. Some might argue the bank was fair, acting within its legal rights. I was tempted to think the same until we stumbled into an unexpected comparative case.

For reasons no one knows, another local church in our community mistakenly sent us their financials. Their position was not materially different from ours. Their growth, giving units, and membership numbers were practically the same as ours. We both were applying for a loan for sanctuary expansion at a local bank. The difference? This other congregation was majority white, and they received a loan while we didn't. We were forced to go searching for a bank outside of our community that didn't have a local public relations tie.

Truth be told, we were accustomed to mistreatment and sleight-of-hand actions of banks in our personal and corporate lives. There is a history that persons of color have not been treated fairly by lending institutions. We experienced this in real time when that other church's financials fell into our lap. We thought we had cleared that hurdle by getting approval for the needed loan from this bank. But even that wasn't enough. Reality set in.

The treatment of our forefathers echoed in our present-day treatment.[4] The players have changed but the game has not—and the consequences are dire. The inequity of capital in a community not only affects the wealth potential of Black and Brown communities but also dramatically curtails the growth of its most treasured and trusted institutions, in particular the church.[5] We get triple hit.[6] We are denied wealth accumulation mechanisms like rapidly rising house values, we get paid less on average for doing the same jobs, and then those reasons are used indirectly to deny us opportunities to grow our institutions.[7]

THE COST OF CHAOS

Chaos has costs. When order is lost, time, talent, and treasure are affected. When that cold winter morning turned my life upside down, I immediately searched to see what I could have done differently. Despite knowing the unfair playing field, I blamed myself. I had failed my people. I was not up to the task, or so the devil was working to tell me. I knew I had to devise a plan for telling the leaders and the congregation and find a way to pick up the pieces to finish the construction project. First, I had to tell the vision board, our version of the church board. While shaken to my core with doubt, hurt, and confusion, I could not be seen shaking. So I stilled myself with prayer and counsel from trusted advisers.

I reached out to three colleagues who have unique roles in my life. Bishop Johnson prayed with me and told me his faith story. I knew he had come to America with a suitcase full of faith and no money. His fervor for souls has resulted in him planting hundreds of churches, principally in Africa as a direct result of his prayer life. He spoke faith into me and prayed with me. Bishop Scott Thomas told me how I needed to raise money in a hurry. He walked me through how I should tell the church about this unjust move by the bank. Another of my spiritual mentors, the first person I called, told me to stop crying because he couldn't understand a word I was saying. My broken heart was speaking broken English, and even he couldn't interpret my tongues. The tears wouldn't stop. I was a shell, a snow globe of emotions shaken with no hope of stability. I told him I was contemplating suicide. I could think of no other way out. All I knew was that I had failed my people and could see no path forward. How could I let this happen?

All three men were there for me without a doubt, but none of them could mend my brokenness or give me what I thought would be a final solution. All I could think about was that people would think I did something wrong. They would think I stole the money. They would think I lied. They would believe the bank over me. They would not believe the city changed the requirements, which changed the amount of money needed. It was a cascade of needs that overwhelmed me and now was breaking me.

The final solution, I thought, would be to take my own life. This would be my last gift to my congregation, as the six-million-dollar insurance policy on my life would pay for the completion of the construction project with money left over for my family to survive my demise. I was not worried about going to hell. I believed God would forgive me for taking my life. I believed my name would be cleared. As a leader, I believed I would have done what leaders do: solve problems and serve people. I was convinced of that.

Hindsight is obvious. I was not thinking clearly at all. My heart was broken, my mind was broken, and I was no longer a whole person. My spirit had cracked and was leaking out on the floor. Yet I felt I couldn't let anyone see my brokenness. A few days later, I stood in my office talking to my spiritual mentor on the phone, just moments before I had to go to the board meeting to tell them what happened. Hearing him say "Stop crying because I can't understand you!" triggered something in me. I told him what I was going to do—kill myself.

His response made me pause, "Who will lead the church if you kill yourself?" At that time, my son was an undergrad at Morehouse College. He was not ready to succeed me. At the time of this conversation, my son and daughter were attending my spiritual mentor's conference for millennials. My mentor stopped what he was doing to come off the platform to take my call and talk me off the ledge. While the thought of the final solution of suicide subsided momentarily, the ideation lingered for years through the chaos. At that moment, however, I wiped my eyes and took wise counsel. I put Visine in my eyes to clear the redness. I stiffened my resolve and told the CFO to assemble the board so that I could lead them through the chaos.

LESSONS LEARNED

The combination of advice I received with my own sense of direction led me to tell the congregation on a Sunday morning what the bank had done and that construction would stop until we could find another lender. After I received advice from men I trusted, I prayed to seek God's wisdom as to how to communicate this chaotic moment. I concluded that I would be transparent and lay it all out on a Sunday morning after worship, a word that was designed to build their faith. This news to the congregation would come after I told that same news to each group of leaders—elders, ministers, deacons, and ministry leaders. It seemed a wise approach at the time, but it wasn't. In fact, it was probably one of the biggest mistakes I made. In my effort to be an ethical leader amid chaos, I stopped leading. I was simply relaying reality when people in such times need more. I should have been a transformational leader, exhibiting inspiration, individualization, intellectualism, and ideology.

According to Bruce Avolio's extensive research, transformational leaders improve the performance of followers. They help their followers reach their fullest potential. People who exhibit transformational leadership often have a strong set of internal values and ideals. They are effective in motivating followers to act in ways that support the greater good rather than their own self-interests. Idealized Influence is the emotional component of leadership. Idealized Influence describes leaders who act as strong role models for followers; followers identify with these leaders and want very much to emulate them.

Inspirational Motivation is descriptive of leaders who communicate high expectations to followers, inspiring them through motivation to become committed to and a part of the shared vision in the organization. In practice, leaders use symbols and emotional appeals to focus group members' efforts to achieve more than they would in their own self-interest.

Intellectual Stimulation includes leadership that stimulates followers to be creative and innovative and to challenge their own beliefs and values as well as those of the leader and the organization.[8]

Individualized Consideration means that leaders provide a supportive climate in which they listen carefully to the individual needs of followers. Leaders act as coaches and advisers while trying to assist followers in becoming fully actualized.[9]

The congregation trusted my leadership. That was proven by the hundreds of thousands of dollars they had given to the project. But I let the fear I felt of a few people not believing in me make me take a Sunday morning to air our "dirty laundry." It is difficult to overstate how treacherous fear can be in such moments. Every leader knows they will have critics. Every leader will be questioned. But to let the fear of a few shape the whole is a mistake we make too often. Be cognizant of this temptation, and flee it. Never forget that the crowd doesn't really care about the weedy details.

In my fear of a few, I failed to anticipate how airing the dirty laundry and my "solution" of requesting that every household contribute $1,000 as soon as possible would change the narrative in the community about the church, and in some instances reinforce other negative narratives. A false narrative had been circulating by some in the larger community through barbershops and hair salons that we were a "prosperity church" always looking for money. I only oxygenated such embers by how I handled the situation with the congregation. The leadership of the church remained fully on board with the vision, but the fear of rejection from the crowd and not the core drove my decision to choose the wrong forum for rallying the church around the desperate moment to continue to build.

It was a mistake to tell the congregation of the problem on a Sunday morning. I should have simply kept holding the vision in front of our community. The church needed a leader who would tap into their individual willingness to be inspired by a cause. They needed a transformational leader who could see past current problems and intellectually grasp the solution. They needed to see a leader who could guide them through strong headwinds and use the wind to fill the church sails. Instead, at best they got a transactional leader who gave them a problem on a Sunday morning then asked them to give $1,000 on Mother's Day. The money did position the church to acquire a loan from another lender. However, the chaos that ensued cost the church much-needed momentum and about 5 percent of our membership. This came on the heels of the executive pastor, the youth pastor, and the minister of music leaving within months of each other.

LEADERSHIP PRINCIPLES

Multiple leadership lessons can be learned through this chaotic gut-wrenching event in the life of New Life Church, but I will focus on three:

1. Leadership theory—knowing which leadership principles to apply
2. Timing—knowing when, where, and whom to share the problems of the church, organization, or individuals you lead with
3. Counsel—getting advice from other senior leaders

Leadership theory. There are literally hundreds of leadership theories, each of which has pluses and minuses. Choose the appropriate one and add it to your authentic self. This approach will bear fruit as you confront various leadership problems and challenges. Keep in mind that you must nimbly choose an effective leadership theory to address the problem in your context, one you and your team will know best. The theory I chose was transformational.

Transformational leadership has four distinct components that translate into actualization. These transforming components are as follows: idealized influence, intellectual stimulation, individualized consideration, and inspirational motivation. This quadrant of leadership theories may seem like high and lofty academic language with no real-world application, but these components have practical meaning. Like the repetition of war games when I was a chaplain in the Air Force sharpened me for warfare, these theories had the potential of being lifted off the pages and becoming a rudder in my storm.

Avolio and Bass suggest leadership is not a transaction between uninvolved individuals but a communal relationship designed to transform each other and the world around them.[10] The interaction of a leader with higher followers changes both for the good. Paul put it this way:

> Don't become so well-adjusted to your culture that you fit into it without even thinking. Instead, fix your attention on God. You'll be changed from the inside out. Readily recognize

what he wants from you, and quickly respond to it. Unlike the culture around you, always dragging you down to its level of immaturity, God brings the best out of you, develops well-formed maturity in you. (Romans 12:1-2 MSG)

Jesus took twelve men and made them idealistic, inspirational, more intellectually astute about the law, and more authentic about their identity.

In the throes of my situation, I could only see a moment of transaction: if the congregation did X, then the results would be the restart of construction. In this reaction, I missed a key moment to transform the community to experience a deeper level of faith. The problems the bank presented were packed with transformational opportunities had I been transformed by the theories I was studying rather than just learning them. I should have worked with my core leaders, pointing them to God and how God permits obstacles to build our faith. God said as much with the children of Israel. He wanted them to see what was in their hearts in the wilderness: "Remember how the LORD your God led you all the way in the wilderness these forty years, to humble and test you in order to know what was in your heart, whether or not you would keep his commands" (Deuteronomy 8:2). What came out of my heart was fear of failure.

Timing. Timing is everything. God's timing is perfect. He knows the end from the beginning. "I make known the end from the beginning, from ancient times, what is still to come. I say, 'My purpose will stand, and I will do all that I please'" (Isaiah 46:10). The senior leader must be in tune with God's timing. This was one of my biggest mistakes. I feared I would lose interest and enthusiasm for the project, so I hurried to tell the congregation news that should have been disseminated in a more deliberate way. A stunning characteristic of Jesus—with the weight of the entire world and all of history on his shoulders—was that he was never in a hurry. I got in a hurry.

With graphs, slides, and PowerPoint presentations, I turned a Sunday morning worship experience into a dog-and-pony show where neither dog nor pony was potty trained. My military precision briefing was professional, but this was not the time to cast problems. I needed to cast visions of solutions. To this day, I deeply regret my bad timing, lack of discernment, and noble but incorrect need to be transparent. That morning became a megaphone to the community: "Don't go to New Life, because they are in trouble."

I continually learn that God's timing is perfect. Pray long and hard as God will tell you when, how, and whom to share the problems of the church/organization/individuals you lead with. "He reveals deep and hidden things; he knows what lies in darkness, and light dwells with him" (Daniel 2:22). It took New Life Church and I years to turn the volume of that narrative down.

Counsel. I correctly reached out to senior leaders to ask what they would do. "Where there is no guidance, a people falls, but in an abundance of counselors there is safety" (Proverbs 11:14 ESV). When you receive counsel, weigh it and make sure the advice fits your context. One piece of advice I got was to do an open journal to my congregation, sharing my innermost thoughts and doubts, like a running editorial of the events as they transpired. Even though this was one way to be transparent and show my vulnerability, this did not fit in my context. It had the opposite effect. My view of myself was I had projected weakness when my congregation needed to see strength—a transformational leader in charge of the situation. Again, I missed the opportunity to transform my community. Instead of laying bare my fears I should have ushered in a realistic moment of sheer faith amid fear. I should have used my senior leadership council as my safe place to park my fears.

Avolio and Bass do not portray the leader as a cult leader to be idolized but a real-world leader to whom followers can idealistically and vicariously relate. Paul led similarly, "Follow me as I follow Christ" (1 Corinthians 11:1 MEV). Paul was an extremely transparent leader, "So I find this law at work: Although I want to do good, evil is right there with me. . . . What a wretched man I am! Who will rescue me from this body that is subject to death?" (Romans 7:21, 24) and consistently transformed those who followed him. The problems I confronted were packed with possibilities for transformation had Avolio and Bass' leadership theory not only been learned but applied.

QUESTIONS FOR REFLECTION AND DISCUSSION

1. What problems are you or your organization experiencing?
2. What counsel have you sought?
3. What mistakes, if any, have been made?
4. What leadership principles/theories could you begin to apply to your situation?

7

CASH

WHEN MONEY IS NOT ENOUGH

*Nothing flows without currency and a purse is doubly
empty when it's full of borrowed money.*

UNKNOWN

I REMEMBER SITTING in the back of my father's small rural church one Sunday morning watching the chairman of the deacon board raise the offering. After we all marched around the offering table and gave our tithes, he counted the money at the table while the worship team played on. With great anticipation, we waited to hear the total. Then came the announcement: "We are only a few dollars from raising one of the best offerings ever, if we can just get everybody else to give again."

The marching began again around the table, this time with fewer people. Then, with even greater fanfare, the chairman announced the new amount and dancing in the Spirit broke out throughout the congregation. God was praised! There was enough to pay for the ministry of the church for another week. This was my introduction to church finances, budgets, and fundraising. Sunday morning is not only a time of corporate worship in the African American community, but also a display of the net worth (available cash on hand) and faith of the people.

NET WORTH

The more things change, the more they stay the same. The way we give has changed. The amount we need has changed. The amount we give has changed. But what has not changed is the per capita net worth of most African American churches. God's work is done by what God's people give, and the church's leader must be resourceful. Outcomes and output are directly connected to the input of the limited dollars in the African American community. Therefore, the net worth of its church members correlates to the level of ministry that will be produced. So for a leader the pressure to do more with less can be intense.

What a church can do is directly connected to the average income and net worth of its giving base. It takes cash, and lots of it, to do a lot of ministry. Ministry uplifts the community it serves. The weight and burden to raise the African American community has traditionally rested on the shoulders of the African American church. Many of the historically Black colleges and universities (HBCUs) were started by the African American church, the most trusted institution in the African American community since Richard Allen refused to sit in the colored section in the balcony at Saint George's Methodist Episcopal Church in Philadelphia in 1787. While the Black church is endeared and trusted with the burden and blessing of lifting its community up, it is handicapped by the historically low net worth of the community it serves. New Life Church is no different.

CASH IS NOT ALWAYS GREEN

New Life Church is situated on the Illinois side of the Mississippi River in the metropolitan area of St. Louis, Missouri. Our congregation is made up of predominantly African Americans from the entire socioeconomic scale. When the leadership of the church decided to expand the size of the sanctuary, our cash could not compete with our color. When we applied for a loan, our cash flow was sufficient and our debt-to-income ratio was within the bank's parameters, but the local banks had redlined us.[1] They decided that the demographic makeup of our church was too much of a risk just as banks have redlined African American neighborhoods since World War II.

Even though we were squarely in a middle- to upper-middle-class community, we were too risky. We found this out the hard way. When we applied for a building permit, we had to overcome the neighbors trying to prevent us from building due to NIMBY ("not in my backyard"). They took us to court, and our lawyer shared with our leadership team the judge's chamber conversation with him and the plaintiffs' lawyer. Someone said, "I thought this was a congregation from down the hill trying to build in O'Fallon."

"Down the hill" is a colloquialism referring to East St. Louis, a predominantly African American and underserved community. This was the nature of New Life's reality and the opposition we contended with as we sought to meet the needs of the growing community of African Americans living "up the hill." It wasn't just about cash. Rather it was cash colored by others' perceptions of our skin tones.

As I mentioned previously, someone had anonymously sent us the financials of a predominantly Caucasian church, which revealed very little difference in our giving units, income, and growth rate. The comparison was a glaring example of net worth not being enough and that the color of cash is not always green: "in this country—the United States—it always keeps returning to race."[2] Given repeatedly unsuccessful applications to area banks, we had no choice but to apply to banks outside of our community to expand our sanctuary and ministry footprint.

It was not our desire to get a loan outside of our bi-state region. Banks tend not to be sensitive to their public relations if they must call the loan. And likely would not want to work things out if the church had a season of low giving. But what caused us to go with the bank we chose was the fact that they approved our loan and seemed eager to have a long-term relationship with us. The covenants they put on the loan seemed reasonable to our lawyer, so we proceeded.

Shortly after construction started, the city changed its ordinances, significantly increasing project costs. Moreover, the bank required us to accept additional covenants that included new capital campaign fundraising benchmarks. They were more aggressive, but our giving was strong and our congregation was motivated. We met two of the three giving benchmarks. It was tough because the congregation had already made pledges and were fulfilling them for the most part. To go back and ask for a second bite of the apple right after the holidays is hard even for a very generous church like ours. But we did it!

After their site visit, the bank verbally communicated that they were satisfied we would meet the third benchmark. We did, although late. Then the bank reneged on their verbal word that turned into a cold day in hell. The fact that the bank officials literally shook our hand and said they would accept our late infusion of capital for the project and then turned around and didn't do it was a slap in our face.

This dishonesty has its roots in racism going all the way back to America's colonial history. We tend to only look at the banking practices of redlining after WWII,[3] practices that continue to have significant effects on communities of color, providing a culture of sleight-of-hand practices by banks.[4] But those practices are structurally connected to the resource distribution that privileged whiteness and white racialized identity.[5] These practices have been canonized in the majority culture seeing the Black church as a threat.[6]

While I am not saying the bankers who turned my life upside down saw me as a physical threat, I am saying their actions are grounded in generations of racism and fear, and irrational emotions often originate from perceived threats. Malcolm Gladwell argues that we all revert to our innate perception of people we don't know, which is the summation of our life experiences, socializations, and upbringing.[7] The end result is often a racist decision, which can be disastrous as it was for me and New Life.

Dr. Michael Emerson puts it this way:

> In the U.S., neighborhoods, housing, organizations, and loan-making are color-coded. It is a complicated process of many and multiple steps, but at each turn, these steps favor white people and organizations and penalize people of color and their organizations. From redlining to the appraisal industry to neighborhood appreciation and depreciation to the assessment of risk, black people and organizations face a far more difficult set of hurdles to receive loans and receive them on reasonable terms than do white people and their organizations.[8]

The bank's decision to rescind the loan instituted a cash crisis for the church. After weeks that turned into months that turned into years of prayer, faith, disappointments, and one turned-down application after another, the church finally got a lender to loan us the money to complete the project. New Life Church overcame that very visible crisis of an incomplete construction project. But there was another storm just over the horizon that was not so apparent.

NEW LOAN

As I shared in a previous chapter, when the construction project stopped my world fell apart. In my constant counsel with my spiritual mentor, and in the midst of my brokenness and tears on a weekly basis, he recommended a church financial adviser, Kenneth and Connie Lewis of Clearinghouse Advisory Group Inc. They are known for rescuing churches that are in dire straits by financing their projects.

We secured their services. They immediately went to work scouring the country for a lender. We applied to more than forty-five banks. Many of the applications went all the way to the underwriting process to include appraisals with mountains of paperwork. The arduous process was literally a twenty-four-hour/seven-days-a-week process that lasted years. Every bank found a reason to say no. It was never due to debt-to-income ratio, cash flow, or the departure of the executive pastor, youth pastor, or worship pastor. It was always due to something they refused to put in writing.[9] Kenneth said that based on his experience, it was not because the other bank pulled out that was being used as an excuse not lend, but the real reason was the color of our skin, not the color of our money, given that our financial surpassed the underwriting criteria.[10] The color of the cash holders clearly mattered. "It always comes down to race in America."[11]

Kenneth said he had one last option. Whenever I hear that phrase, I know I am in for a troubling time. My initial gut reaction was not to proceed, praying that another option would emerge. It didn't, so we did our due diligence on the last option. The new lender seemed to show concern about our plight. In every due-diligence meeting, they assured us they would fund the project to completion. We laid the project out, hired a new contractor and even a construction manager at the request of the new lender, which significantly increased the cost of the project. The new lender seemed to have kingdom building at heart and a complete understanding of our journey—so we were led to believe.

Church loans are different from regular business loans. They fall into the same category in that the bank is not lending to an individual, but they are different because a church building generally does not hold a lot of value to be collateralized, and the service the church sells only generates a freewill offering. These facts make banks extra cautious in lending to churches. Because the church building falls into the category of a special-use building, which limits the number of potential buyers should the bank have to foreclose, banks really do view the loan as a cash basis loan even though they never say that in the underwriting process. In other words, lenders ask if there is more than enough cash flow and revenue to cover their loans and mitigate their risk. The cash flow of the church is directly connected to the net worth of its congregants.

Therefore, when a church of color that has been secretly redlined reapplies after a bank pulled out of the project, it is perceived by lenders as "super high risk." When a lending institution takes a high-risk loan, the commensurate terms are adjusted to mitigate the risk. This is a nice way of saying we got a lender who was nothing more than a church lender with payday-loan proclivities—a wolf in sheep's clothing. They knew we had no other options. We knew we had no other options. An incomplete construction project is a sign of failure and unattractive to possible new members. Something had to be done. So, after consultation with our vision board, my mentors, and a whole lot of prayer, I signed the promissory note.

In the beginning, the lending institution presented itself as the savior of churches who had found themselves in a construction project mess at no fault of their own. The lenders assured us in person and on paper that their purpose and passion were to help build the kingdom of God. They said they existed for no other business purpose. To show their fidelity to our cause they offered to take my family and me to a Dallas Cowboys game. Being a Cowboys fan, I considered this invitation a no-brainer. I should have known something was up when our promised box seats turned into nosebleed seats in the end zone.

Construction restarted at an increased project cost. We were in a relationship with a lender who promised in writing they would never leave us or forsake us, but my trust was grossly misplaced. I soon learned our lender was a Dr. Jekyll who would turn into a Mr. Hyde. All the promises crumbled under the weight of another change order in the construction. When I was able to convince another construction company to take over what the previous company had left, they added to their rough order of magnitude (ROM) estimates, which calculate the probable cost of the project. This was reasonable since they would have to finish another company's work and put their reputation on the line. When the price went up again on top of the lender, requiring us to have a project manager, we did not have enough cash to finish the project. But the lender promised in writing to lend what it took. Promises, it appears, were made to be broken.

BROKEN IN PIECES

Here I was again. The weight of the world was back. Sweat-filled, sleepless nights. Grinding my teeth while sleeping. Questioning myself constantly. The fragility of my marriage. What was left of me was broken. Trapped in my decisions, like a mouse cornered by a cat and by a person with a broom ready to take me out. Almost one million dollars more to finish the project. The lender promised they would lend the money to cover the cost. They put it in a letter of commitment that the construction company used to start the project.

My wife and I had planned the anniversary trip of a lifetime and were looking forward to traveling to London, Paris, then to Dubai. I had bought her a yellow diamond ring, and I planned to propose to her all over again at dinner in the tallest building in the world in Dubai. Instead, after receiving counsel from my spiritual mentor that such a lavish trip would be unseemly during construction, especially if we had to disclose for a second time that construction had to stop, that decision put an even more severe strain on my marriage. Now, regular middle-aged couple disagreements of empty nest and other norms had become exacerbated. My bride's sacrifices were also straining her to the breaking point. There was no more left of me to break. I could not even celebrate my bride.

I canceled the trip. I took the ring back. After nights of anguish and days of walking dead, I made a life-altering decision: I used my retirement fund to keep the project going. I couldn't tell the church because another hit would have emptied us. I did what I believed a leader should do—solve problems. Now I was broken in more ways than one. While this infusion of cash kept things going, bills kept rising and the lender kept promising to pay the rest at completion of construction. The sacrifices leaders make take a toll on marriages and family as well as ministry. Holding it together required my broken herculean effort every day.

The retirement money provided just enough cash flow to complete the construction, and joy was everywhere. We had a marching band in the sanctuary. The praise dancers followed. People were everywhere. The community narrative was changing back to positives. The ribbon was cut, but the bills were due, lien waivers had to be cleared, and then the sky fell: the lender reneged—to this day, they have never said why. It is consistent with the treatment of Black churches by lending institutions.[12] Because the construction company has such an integral reputation, they gave us the keys, but the completed construction project bills were due. Now we had a mortgage and construction bills to pay.

There was not much of me left to lead, but that didn't matter. Problems have to be solved. Sermons have to be preached. Lives have to be discipled. Leaders don't bleed on their followers. They stand at the door of the fold like Jesus and bind up their wounds when they come and go. There was less of me when we marched in because I knew our reality, and I didn't have a lot of money left. Now the final solution of taking my life was not just an idea. I was broken in every way, but I still had to pull it together and lead and preach and be a father and husband and not bleed on the people. I did a good job binding everybody's wounds but mine until my emotional dam broke.

ROBBING PETER TO PAY PAUL

As all of this was going on, I received a coveted preaching appointment from my seminary friend Bishop Kim Brown, whose church had grown into a megachurch. I was overjoyed at the chance to preach there, but it couldn't have come at a worse time. I was barely able to write sermons for my congregation because all I could hear ringing in my spirit were the constant phone calls and emails from the mortgage lender that was not going to honor their commitment. The construction company wanted their money, and the mortgage company wanted their money. We had not budgeted to pay both.

The lender for construction was now also the mortgage company. Normally, that wouldn't be a problem, but they didn't lend enough money to pay for construction. Had they, we would have had the standard twenty-year amortized payment. Instead, they threw around the word *foreclosure* to beat me into submission. I was beyond angry and broken. They were the reason Peter and Paul were not always getting what they wanted every month. I swung between anger and despair over the situation, but I refused to tell the church because this was not something you could explain on a Sunday morning. You cannot bleed on the people.

I had learned my lesson—just cast the vision. But the weight was far too heavy now because construction bills were due as well as the mortgage, and all my retirement savings were gone. I was using my son's college fund to make sure the church paid Peter and Paul. I refused to beg for money on Sunday morning. Nothing runs people away from a church faster than if people think it's all about a money grab. So, my final solution seemed permissible—take my life so that the keyman life insurance policy would pay for everything. But oddly preaching for my seminary buddy was something I could still look forward to.

I flew to my friend's church having just received a doomsday phone call from the lender, who was refusing to pay for all the construction and again threatened foreclosure on a building they never fully paid to construct. One minute I was thinking about my sermon, and the next minute I was worrying about our mortgage. The terms of the loan were hitting and just like a payday loan, the tactics were ruthless. On top of all of that, just before I left, my wife and I had a huge argument. The stress of ministry was beginning to break our marriage.

When I checked into the hotel, I stood at the window and decided that this was it. No more. I couldn't let the lender's threats of foreclosure become a reality. I had to end my life to preserve the congregation's life. But it was at that moment God stepped in. The phone rang. It was Bishop Walter Scott Thomas, my executive coach, returning my call. I had been calling him to help me strategize my way out. I was standing at the window, wondering if the fifth floor was high enough for my exit strategy. I didn't want to be maimed. I needed the landing to be final so that the insurance would pay out.

Then Bishop Thomas said something profound to me that forever crushed the power the final solution had over me: "If you do commit suicide, you will never know how the Lord was going to bring you out." His words were piercing. They had to come straight from heaven because he knew nothing of my struggle with suicide ideation until I told him while standing at the window looking at where I would land. I was solving the problem rather than relying on God. His words caused the crumbs of my soul to gather, resonating with me.

I turned away from the window. The drumbeat of foreclosure, two major bills a month, and a strained marriage continued, but I stopped dancing to its beat. Let God be the drum major. My wife and I had been meeting with a counselor to deal with the strain on our marriage, so when I shared my suicidal ideation in a session, the therapist made us a priority. I also sought individual therapy where my therapist helped me identify my need for perfection and my fear of failure. Each session dug deeper into how my need to be a superhero was connected to my desire to be accepted. Accomplishing great things and walking the high wire of risk would garner me words of affirmation, which is the antidote. I felt isolated. I didn't feel like I could share that with anyone. In hindsight, I should have shared the problems if not my suicidal ideation. Somehow twisted in my mind, suicide would mean I would be known as the pastor who sacrificed it all for his flock. My therapist helped me see Jesus had already died for the church.

LEADERSHIP LESSONS LEARNED

During this cash-challenged time, despite my weaknesses and near-fatal flaw, I attempted to be a servant leader. There are ten pillars on which the theory of servant leadership rests: listening, empathy, healing, awareness, persuasion, conceptualization, foresight, stewardship, commitment to the growth of the people, and building community.[13] A servant leader sees himself or herself as secondary to the growth and development of others. Community development is paramount, and accomplishing the mutual goals of the community becomes a preoccupation as well.[14]

I endeavored to be sensitive to the concerns of the congregation by intensifying my prayer life. Any stoppage in construction would have been intolerable. In my mind, it was almost as if the congregation said, "Don't restart if we are not going to finish it." Therefore, I constantly placed myself in the shoes of the LifeChangers. *Should they know we had once again started and stopped and been taken advantage of by a dishonest lender?* I thought.

I wanted my congregation to heal from the bank pulling out, key staff leaders leaving, and damage to a sterling reputation for being the church that people want to go to. Aware of our limitations, I pulled too many things onto myself. When I returned from my preaching engagement with Bishop Brown, I shared with the executive board of the vision board the financial weight of whom to pay. The executive board stepped up and doubled—even tripled—their personal giving. They used their influence with others in the church, encouraging them to give more to alleviate the financial stress. When I shared with the executive board members what I was doing personally, they encouraged me to never take that on myself again. They came along side me like Aaron and Hur and held up my arms (Exodus 17:10-13). They were surprised to hear the weight of the moment and that I had pulled it on myself and the director of operations to manage alone.

From then on, they surrounded me with support, encouragement, wise counsel, and strategy sessions to overcome the challenges. Even though they made it clear they needed me to share the weight of ministry, I never shared my suicide ideations. With their help my foresight and conceptualization of how to solve the cash problems grew by leaps and bounds. Oddly enough, my sharing the burden with my key leadership started slowly turning things around. Our stewardship of cash became easier because there was more of it. Through prayer and strategic stewardship campaigns at the beginning of the year, we were able to satisfy Peter and Paul.

All too often within the body of Christ, we look at servant leaders as the quintessential biblical model of leadership.

> Jesus called them together and said, "You know that the rulers of the Gentiles lord it over them, and their high officials exercise authority over them. Not so with you. Instead, whoever wants to become great among you must be your servant, and whoever wants to be first must be your slave—just as the Son of Man did not come to be served, but to serve, and to give his life as a ransom for many." (Matthew 20:25-28)

In this Scripture, Jesus makes it clear his disciples should be servant leaders, but there is a thin line between serving the body of Christ as Jesus did and serving them as a Savior. There is only one Savior (Hebrews 10:12). There is no need to be another sacrifice. Jesus has already died for the church. We don't have to.

As servant leaders, we serve believers best when we empower them by pointing them to Jesus and not by falling into a hero complex. Because pastors and church leaders tend to have a serve-at-all-cost mindset, they can fall prey to their own devices. The church has one Savior, and he said, "On this rock I will build my church" (Matthew 16:18). It won't fail. To that end, the ten pillars of a servant leader are fulfilled when the leader serves within the restraints of his or her humanity and is attentive to his or her limitations via self-leadership.

QUESTIONS FOR REFLECTION AND DISCUSSION

1. When you find yourself under financial or budgeting strains what are your strategies?
2. What are your stress triggers? What coping strategies do you employ when you are stressed?
3. If you have thoughts of harming yourself, help is available. Call the Suicide and Crisis Lifeline (9-8-8) or Emergency (9-1-1).

8

COMMUNITY

FROM "HOSANNA!" TO "CRUCIFY HIM!"

"But for what crime?" But they yelled all the louder, "Nail him to a cross!"

MARK 15:14 MSG

JESUS' TRIUMPHANT ENTRY into Jerusalem days before his death is recorded in the Synoptic Gospels (Matthew 21:6-10; Mark 11:6-11; Luke 19:34-44). All three provide details about Jesus' story from the palms waving and cloaks on the ground to shouts of "Hosanna!" Often, we think of the crowd of the Palm Sunday sermon and the crowd in the Easter Sunday sermon as one and the same. While it makes for good preaching, synthesizing both crowds as one that turned its back on Jesus when he needed them the most, there is no empirical data for this. In our minds, our hermeneutics, and our beliefs, the same people who said "Hosanna!" also said "Crucify him!" Based on Jesus' experience that week though, it didn't matter. Whether it was the same people was not as important as the narrative in the community. It was their narrative. Whether it was one crowd, two combined, or even a whole new crowd, the gathered community was telling Jesus the current narrative about him.

I quickly learned I could not chase down rumors and lies about me and New Life Church. The old saying is true: a lie can circle the globe twice before the truth gets out of bed. Who said what is of no value in the investigation, but the narrative in the community is what matters the most. It was not the mere three words "Hosanna!" and "Crucify him" that killed Jesus. It was the narrative in the streets that killed Jesus.

> Then the chief priests and the Pharisees called a meeting of the Sanhedrin. "What are we accomplishing?" they asked. "Here is this man performing many signs." ... "You do not realize that it is better for you that one man die for the people than that the whole nation perish." (John 11:47, 50)

The narrative in the streets is what spurred the chief priest and Pharisees into action to kill Jesus. The narrative in the community will either grow or kill a church or organization. While ministry should not be orchestrated to the tunes of the narratives on the streets, ignoring them is not wise either. I learned the narrative about New Life Church was changing.

WORD ON THE STREET

Jesus had two years of popularity from the moment he turned water into wine to healing the man at the pool of Bethesda, then a year of opposition. Interestingly, in the latter year of opposition, Jesus was interested in the word on the street about him. Jesus wanted to know the narrative in the community. "Who do people say the Son of Man is?" (Matthew 16:13). Whether it is Jesus' humanity asking the question or his divinity leaving breadcrumbs for us to learn from, the curiosity of what people are saying about you is a lesson God wants us to learn from.

The answer was quick in coming. Peter spoke up with authority, as usual, and was right and wrong within minutes. There will always be something said about you as a leader in the public forum.

As with Jesus, it will be a mixture of truth and falsehood, but in both cases, Jesus was not swayed by public opinion. He easily put the accolades of men behind him. Even at the point of death in his dialogue with Pilate, Jesus is not moved by the people's characterization of who he is and what he has done. Apart from the prophetic reality of the moment, this exchange could have saved Jesus if he was moved by the narrative of people, even powerful people like Pilate. But he wasn't (John 18:33-38, 40).

New Life Church faced a similar narrative. The word on the street shifted from the moment I told the church the bank pulled out on us and then asked for $1,000 per family. That was a costly decision, though it was the right financial decision, because our balance sheet improved, but it hurt our narrative on the street. Choices in ministry are not always good, better, and best. Sometimes they are bad and worst. New Life was twelve years old when our years of popularity began to wane. The word on the street had begun to show signs of negativity two years before when key staff members resigned. The bank pullout was like the little boy who had his finger in the levee and then pulled it out and all the water flooded the village. It didn't matter whether it was "Hosanna!" or "Crucify him!" or who was saying it. The shift was happening, and the storm was raging.

The narrative change can feel like being seasick. My first bout with seasickness was when I was at my first base as a chaplain. I decided to take the men's ministry on a deep-sea fishing trip. I had never been on a rowboat let alone out in the middle of the ocean in a fishing boat. The idea was to get the men interested in the chapel service. It wasn't long into the trip before I was so sick that I pleaded with Jesus to stop my swimming head, promising he would never have to hear this prayer again if he would just get me to the shore. The narrative on the street was a similar experience for me.

It's bad enough that the storm is raging in your ministry, but then you add the fact that everybody is talking about it. While my suicidal ideation was dead my PTSD was not. Fear of rejection and public embarrassment can be a death sentence to one's well-being. So I went back to the counselor for more therapy. We discussed my triggers and how to mitigate their effect on me. PTSD affects your equilibrium. It affects the way you think. Like seasickness, all you can think about is getting to the seashore. Catching fish is no longer important. Survival becomes paramount.

I felt like there was no stable place to stand. I was off balance again, but this time I had help navigating the storms. My therapy sessions helped me to see my walk was not unlike that of Peter walking on water. I was not walking on water, but I was looking at the wind instead of Jesus who was in arm's reach of the boat. After Jesus reached down and pulled Peter up from the stormy waters they got into the boat, which means they were closer to the boat than Peter knew (Matthew 14:22-33). My sessions helped me see that narratives trigger my fears, but Jesus is close enough to pull me into the security of the boat.

So with every casual errand run, it felt like I saw somebody who used to go to New Life. I didn't know how to approach them. Were they a part of the "Hosanna!" crowd or the "Crucify him" crowd? Should I ask why I hadn't seen them since the storm started, or was it best to say hello and talk about the weather? Besides, who wants to hear someone say, "I heard . . ." or "Well no, pastor, my family and I don't attend your church anymore"? When you are already dizzy, your stomach churning, and you're close to throwing up, it's best to greet one another with a nod and keep it moving. Narrative shifts in the community can seem unmanageable. How do you lead through it? In addition to knowing Jesus is on board do the following.

LESSONS LEARNED

When I was stationed at Moody Air Force Base in Georgia, my first duty station as a chaplain, my boss used to tell me, "The more you stir in sh-t, the more it will stink." His admonition was clear: leave a bad narrative alone. Don't keep talking about it. Stop chasing rumors, innuendos, and misinformation. At the time, I thought he just didn't want to face down his opposition or use his considerable rank to correct the record. I later learned the wisdom of his statement. Sometimes it's best to do as Jesus did. Many times, he would warn people against telling others he was the Christ. It wasn't the right time. This was the first in a series of lessons I experienced.

Jesus remained focused through the years of opposition to his ministry. From Nazareth to Capernaum to Bethsaida to feed the five thousand (Matthew 9:35; Mark 6:35-44), Jesus remained focused. From there he walked on water on the lake with the disciples (Matthew 14:25) and traveled on to Phoenicia to heal the sick daughter of a Greek woman (Mark 7:25-30). His focus took him to the Decapolis where he healed a demon-possessed deaf mute (Matthew 7:32-37). Jesus' focus took him on a boat trip to and from Dalmanutha (Mark 8:10), to heal a blind man (Mark 8:22-26), to Caesarea Philippi (Matthew 16:13), and to the Mount of Transfiguration (Matthew 17:24).

These events took place during Jesus' years of opposition when the narrative had shifted. At no point did Jesus take the off-ramps available because they offended him. He continued to fish for people and heal them. The last thing I felt like doing when I got seasick on the deep-sea fishing boat with the chapel's men's ministry was fish. Jesus leaves a better example. The shifting winds of a community narrative should never change the course once you set sail. To stay focused requires handles to pull yourself up on—faith, prayer, counsel, consecration, and therapy, to name a few.

The second lesson I learned is that storms, no matter how catastrophic, have an expiration date. It didn't feel like it at the time. For nearly ten years the storm raged, and my seasickness got worse and worse. When I was in the thick of it and the community opinion shifted, I had to realize patience and perseverance instead of pursuing people to prove them wrong was a handy tool in my toolchest.

In addition to using patience and perseverance as my tools to get through, I held on to some key verses of Scripture such as James 1:2-4, Galatians 6:9, and finally Romans 5:3-5.

Third, I found my prayer life became a comfort and strength. My mother never saw New Life, but she taught me how to pray and I believe her prayers for my success in ministry lingered in heaven until it was time for God to answer them (Revelation 5:8). Prayers don't dissipate or evaporate. God never acts as if we are not talking to him, but he does respond in his timing. My mother's prayers did not die with her. They lived until God deciphered her cry.

At Brown University doctors have developed computer programs that discern the cries of babies, attaching meaning to them.[1] So it is with our cries to God. God knows the difference between our hungry cry, hurt cry, need-a-change cry, and I-can't-take-it-any-longer cry. When the cries move God, relief comes (1 Corinthians 10:13). My prayers united with my mother's prayers to get me through the shift from "Hosanna!" to "Crucify him!"

Fourth, empowering my leaders was critical. I met with my core leaders regularly instead of waiting until our annual leadership summit. These sessions strengthened the resolve of my core leaders. My philosophy was believing that by strengthening my leaders, they would encounter people I would never come across and defend the church with truth that would set people free from negative narratives. They could combat misinformation with truth. This may sound like asking leaders to chase lies, but it was empowering them to live out the truth of Scripture: "Always be prepared to give an answer to everyone who asks you to give the reason for the hope that you have" (1 Peter 3:15).

Fifth, ever since my days as a chaplain I have preached sermon series. This discipline keeps me focused on the vision or theme for the year. This homiletical approach kept me from bleeding on the people or attacking people from the pulpit. The feeling of hurt, injustice, and rejection can manifest in multiple ways. The pulpit is a place of power. It is easy to fall into the trap of using Sunday as the bully pulpit to spur out your hurt. My long-held discipline of preaching sermon series averted these moments.

Sixth, the wonderful thing about the triumphant entry is it ends in the resurrection. Yes, there must be a crucifixion before there can be a resurrection, but the resurrection makes the "Crucify him" a part of the story rather than the whole story. Because of the resurrection, the Bible ends better than any bedtime story. If a church is truly carrying out the mission of Jesus, there is a strong likelihood it will have people from both crowds crying, Hosanna!" or "Crucify him!" The more involved in the community a church or organization is, the more likely the community story will have interesting chapters about it.

New Life Church is very involved in the community, so the risk of bad press is always prevalent. But remaining focused on fishing for souls, praying, persevering, mixing vision with a gospel message from the pulpit, and not pursuing personal vindication will ensure a resurrection. In the African American community, the Black church is a part of the fabric of the community's existence. The Black community and the Black church are almost synonymous. So "Hosanna!" and "Crucify him!" are equally heartfelt in both settings for good reason—the paths of the Black community and Black church are intertwined, both past and future. We have a vested interest in each other's success. One depends on the other.

LEADERSHIP PRINCIPLES

One of the leadership principles that best illuminates the leader's approach to the shifting storm winds of the community is a behavioral approach. This approach focuses in on the behavior or how the leader navigates public criticism. How does he or she show up when all eyes are on the triumphant entry of the church or organization? How about when those eyes turn from approval to disapproval? The behavioral response of the leader becomes paramount. The leader is in a petri dish and under the microscope at the same time. The leader's behavior must include successfully managing relationships of the community stakeholders, church stakeholders, and church or organization members. Responding to every criticism can cause more problems than it solves.[2]

Church and community stakeholders are critical to carrying out the vision and mission of the church, but pursuing negativity only breeds more and keeps your mind on the negative and not faith. Faith comes by hearing God's Word reverberate in your spirit. Standing firm in the face of an onslaught of criticism is a virtue that can help turn the tide to truth, sometimes without ever saying a word. Managing one's criticism is a behavior followers look for and follow. Jesus is the prime example.

QUESTIONS FOR REFLECTION AND DISCUSSION

1. What is your instinctive response to criticism about your leadership?
2. What are some specific ways you deal with feelings of rejection?
3. How do you empower followers when your church or organization comes under criticism from the community?

PART 4

AFTER THE STORM

9

COUNSELING

IT'S OKAY TO ASK FOR HELP

> *Where there is no [wise, intelligent] guidance, the people fall [and go off course like a ship without a helm], but in the abundance of [wise and godly] counselors there is victory.*
>
> Proverbs 11:14 AMP

THE DAY WAS NOT MUCH DIFFERENT from any other stressful day. I was trying to forge my way out of the mounting problems. The chatter in the community was reverberating in the echo chamber of my mind, like a train rumbling along railroad tracks. I had called my executive coach earlier that week, as I had a vision board meeting coming up and I needed to solidify our strategy to manage the mountain of problems and keep from bleeding on the congregation. I was feeling lower than my usual self. I had become used to feelings of despair. They were familiar unwelcomed friends that kept me company, constantly reminding me that this looming feeling would never forsake me.

While standing at the gas tank pumping gas my phone rang. Finally, my executive coach, Bishop Walter Scott Thomas, was returning my call. I shared with him my despair and desperate need for a congruent strategy to share with my vision board. I told him I was feeling "some kind of way" that I couldn't seem to shake. It was like it had me in a full-nelson wrestling hold, ready to slam me to the cheers of everyone in the church and community. I knew that everyone wasn't against me, but that is not how I felt. I didn't know quite how I felt other than it had become a feeling that was taking up space in my emotions without paying the rent.

Bishop Thomas said, "You feel like a failure. You feel like you have failed your church." I froze. A chill went down my back and tears welled in my eyes. I began to empty out emotions that up to that time I had no name for. Failure—that was it! The trauma and fear of failure. My deep need to be accepted, to be liked and loved for the ministry work I was doing. I hadn't heeded Jesus' warning that when you desire the affirmation of people, you have your reward (Matthew 6:2). That gas tank moment tapped into my empty emotional tank. I couldn't stop the tears. I quickly got into my car to keep from being seen in public crying like a baby.

That gas station conversation caused my past to be gaslighted with years of pent-up negative emotion. I hadn't felt that level of emotion since I was the co-captain of my 24-1 high school basketball team. Everyone blamed me for the one loss. I got a technical foul called on me during a critical moment in the game. We were the favorites against Raleigh Broughton, a team we had never played. Instead, they came into our gym and beat us. To this day, the city of Goldsboro, North Carolina, does not recognize the loss, but everybody remembers who lost it. I felt like a failure for years.

I hadn't let myself feel that feeling since one of my brothers and sisters, next to me in age, called me a derogatory name for the whole summer and refused to play with me, for the whole summer, when we were in grade school. I hadn't felt that feeling of rejection since when my mother took my siblings and I out of the all-Black schools in the sixties and put us in the integrated schools, where we were more often than not, the only Black children in our classes. The feeling of being called names, ignored, and put down for nothing more than being human with an extra dose of melanin from God.

I recognized that feeling when it snuck up on me in an accelerated master's in human relations class during my military service. The professor had us watch *The Eye of the Storm* by Jane Elliott.[1] I had never seen the film about how Elliott, a teacher, devised an experiment to teach her white students the injustice of racism. She divided up the class by their eye color and then treated them differently based on their groupings. Brown eyes were treated like African Americans during the heated days of racism in the sixties and blue eyes were treated like whites. This revolutionary experiment opened her students' eyes and helped open the eyes of the country during the turbulent sixties.

When I finished the film, I broke down in tears in the class. I never knew the negative impact my integrated education experience had on me until then. Since then, I had suppressed the feeling of failure, rejection, and public defaming. I suppressed my siblings' rejection. I suppressed the technical foul costing our team the game. The gas station moment filled me with what my therapist and I had been successfully dealing with and in one moment PTSD kicked in and pinned me to the mat.

I had suppressed that feeling for years and with a lifelong list of victories, a happy marriage, two grown children in ministry, and a decorated career as a chaplain lieutenant colonel, I thought I had defeated that feeling with those personal accomplishments. Now I was the pastor of an undefeated congregation, the talk of the town and facing what seemed like a certain defeat. Public humiliation would be my cause. Once again, I felt the weight of failure in leadership. Another technical foul was about to take me out of the game.

As the tears ran down my face, I quickly drove off talking to Bishop Thomas. He realized he had uncovered a deep emotional wound, so he listened. I didn't realize until later the root of my anguished reached so far back. I was too busy feeling the pain. As Bishop Thomas listened, he began to tell me how to navigate the moment. He said, "You are not what you feel! Your feelings are real, but they are not the real you." He told me to read what God says about me in Scripture. So I found passages and I read them. Deuteronomy 28:13, 1 Samuel 16:7, Psalm 139:14, Romans 8:31, 2 Corinthians 5:17, 2 Corinthians 12:9, and Ephesians 1:4 were particularly helpful to me.

He also told me to read what the men's ministry said to me. As a part of my Father's Day celebration, my executive assistant suggested the men write me a personal card, put some money in it, and tell me what they thought of me and my leadership. She had recognized without knowing all the details of the church challenges I needed a pick-me-up. Words of affirmation is one of my love languages. The men did just that. They didn't say I was a failure. They said I was their leader and that they would follow me anywhere Christ was leading me. Their words energize me to this day.

- "Bishop when I first came to this church your sermon about David and Bathsheba hooked me."
- "Bishop, I look up to you."
- "Bishop, I see how you lead your family and I want to lead like that."
- "You are a man's man, a leader's leader."
- "You are anointed to lead."
- "Thanks for being there for me."

COUNSELING

Bishop Thomas's words of counsel helped me to tap into a latent pain like emotional shingles that had been lying dormant for years. It is critical for those who give counseling to also receive it. There is a reason doctors don't practice on themselves. You may know what's wrong with you and you may not. Either way, you are in no position to prescribe the appropriate medicine. Physician, heal thyself. Senior pastor, heal thyself. Neither work very well.

As a chaplain, I was fortunate to participate in continuing education classes at the Air Force chaplain school that tilled the ground for me to be comfortable with receiving counseling. The emphasis on professional development and self-care was a part of the culture. Unlike the denomination I came out of, a pastor in need of counseling was not frowned on. Military chaplains were one of the main avenues for service members to receive emotional and spiritual care. There was an expectation that if you need counseling for your own mental health, then get it. I entered civilian ministry with that in mind.

When my executive coach gave language to my pain, we agreed I needed counseling. An executive coach is not a counselor. Even though they may be trained in the discipline, their purpose is to help with strategy. It just so happened I already had a counselor because of the wear and tear of ministry on my marriage and family life. Leadership can be draining, exhausting, and taxing, so voices other than friends were needed to maintain some sense of familial equilibrium.

Leaders are passionate and focused about what they believed they have been called to do. This myopic view of life can cause them not to see the needs of their family. If they are not careful everything else can start to come before the family, especially when the everything else is accomplishing the vision they believe God gave them. Leaders have to remember Jesus is the church's bridegroom.

Jesus sought counsel from his heavenly Father. He said that he did not do anything outside of what the Father told him to do. When Jesus struggled with whether to do his will or his Father's will, he saw his friends were not reliable. "Then Jesus went with them to a place called Gethsemane, and he said to his disciples, 'Sit here, while I go over there and pray.' . . . Then he came to the disciples and said to them, 'Sleep and take your rest later on'" (Matthew 26:36, 45 ESV). This passage of Scripture is one of my favorites because it shows the humanity of Jesus and the grace of God in the heart-wrenching moments. Jesus' humanity wanted his friends to help him in his hour of need, like most of us want help in our dark hours. But Jesus also rose to the moment with the help of his heavenly Father. This is consistent with leadership moments.

Bishop's words of counsel were not enough. I needed more. I needed professional therapy. I remember when I was in my clinical pastoral education class in seminary, the professor said our true fears come to the fore in life and death situations. My ministry challenges often felt like life and death situations, and often they were coupled with marriage, family stress, and pain. My therapist encouraged me to turn to prayer, just like Jesus. My prayer life has always been a source of comfort for me. Research shows it is one of the leading tools for ministry leaders to deal with therapeutic healing.[2]

In addition to prayer, therapy helped me to see I lead an unhealthy lifestyle. Juggling and multitasking defers healing and increases opportunities for traumatic gas station episodes.

> Pastoral leaders often keep unhealthy and unsustainable schedules and receive inadequate compensation particularly in comparison to their professional counterparts. The weight of the ministry alone lends itself to stress and burnout if the leader is not careful to maintain adequate self-care. If unaddressed trauma is present along with all of the stressors

commonly found in the life of a ministerial leader, it can profoundly affect not only the leader but the church, ministry, or organization as a whole. Essentially, it can prove to be too much to bear and affect every area of a leader's life, to their demise as well as those they lead and the church, ministry or organization they serve.[3]

I am a work in progress, and my imperfections are still glaring with respect to work and self-help balance. This is why I still have a therapist. We regularly deal with my needs for gratification, love, acceptance, and the elixir of a list of accomplishments.

Jesus sought the counsel of the Father because there was no one else he could turn to for advice. It is extremely important you seek the right person for professional counsel. This was the mistake Saul made. When he was highly distressed and searching for answers, he made the fatal error of going to the wrong person for counsel, and it cost him dearly.

> And when Saul inquired of the LORD, the LORD did not answer him, either by dreams, or by Urim, or by prophets. Then Saul said to his servants, "Seek out for me a woman who is a medium, that I may go to her and inquire of her." And his servants said to him, "Behold, there is a medium at En-dor." (1 Samuel 28:6-7 ESV)

Scripture is replete with instructions to find wise counsel and not to be wise in your own eyes (Proverbs 3:5).

The gas station moment reminded me of several things:

1. Post-traumatic stress is real and you don't need to have been in combat to suffer from it. Trauma can find its way into your inner being.[4] If you don't get help, it can ambush you when you least expect it.

2. Professional help can assist you with getting in touch with your emotions. Healthy emotional intelligence is critical in leadership.

3. The emotional mental health of the leader is just as important as physical health. No one expects a broken bone to heal without a splint. Neither can a broken spirit be healed without the proper care and attention.

LEADERSHIP PRINCIPLE

To lead well, leaders must recognize when they need self-care. Getting professional counseling is directly connected to self-leadership. Knowing how to lead yourself is an often-overlooked area of leadership development. Self-leadership is the term used to describe this phenomenon of understanding and managing ourselves: our strengths, weaknesses, emotions, decisions, responses, words, choices, and relationships. Self-leadership is taking responsibility for ourselves in a way that positions us to assume the responsibility of effectively caring for and leading others.[5]

The emotionally intelligent person is skilled in four areas: identifying emotions, using emotions, understanding emotions, and regulating emotions.[6] If we do not learn to recognize and manage our emotions, we are more likely to respond to others in ways that damage relationships. It is important to take time to process our emotions and think about how we want to respond when there are strong feelings present. Avoid sending a text message, posting on social media, or responding to someone when you have strong feelings like anger, frustration, or disappointment. Instead, you might write the message but wait until the next day to review and send it when your emotions have subsided. You could also walk away and come back to a conversation a few hours later. In many cases, you will find yourself rewriting the message or responding to the conversation differently.

Emotional intelligence has been broken down into four skill areas or domains. Let's focus primarily on the first skill, which is self-awareness.[7] This includes the ability to identify your emotions as they are happening and understanding your personality, strengths, and weaknesses. It is knowing what situations are likely to trigger positive or negative emotions for you. This first skill of self-awareness is critical to the second skill, which is self-management. Once we can anticipate and identify our emotions, we are better able to manage them.

Self-management is creating habits and developing disciplines that allow us to manage our emotions rather than letting our emotions always dictate our words and actions.

LESSONS LEARNED

I learned that the pain of rejection can affect how a person leads. Many pastors have a proclivity toward people pleasing. Because leaders tend to want to be liked they are vulnerable to doing what they can to avoid the feeling of rejection. If they are not healthy emotionally, they may want people to follow them for the wrong reasons. By nature, leadership requires followers, which makes it an easy outlet for searching for acceptance. The process of getting people to follow lends itself to trying to get people to accept you. My episode at the gas station exposed all of that. Thank God I was receptive to counseling and help was at hand.

I also learned the value of self-leadership. In the Air Force, you had to learn how to give first aid to your fellow wounded airmen as well as yourself. During chemical warfare exercises, you had to learn how to put your gas mask on first then check your buddy to make sure their mask was on correctly. The key was to take care of yourself first. Lead yourself first and then lead others. If leaders are not careful, they will lead everyone but themselves. Self-leadership is critical. You cannot save or lead someone else if you have not taken care of yourself first.

We give little thought to annual physicals and getting the blood work done that goes along with that health checkup. Added to our self-preservation and leadership should be an annual mental health checkup. It's putting your oxygen mask on first. It's letting someone else in close enough to expertly ask how you are doing really. The second thing you can do if you have a family is put the oxygen mask on them. Make it a family checkup. Third, talk openly and candidly about how the brain is an organ that needs attention. When this is done you build familial culture and church culture that accepts therapy as a part of life. Finally, preach sermon series on mental health. Elijah under the broom tree, Judas' suicide, and Jacob wrestling with God are a few biblical stories to highlight. It's okay if you're not okay sometimes.

PRACTICAL STEPS

1. Look for a professional therapist just like you would a primary care doctor.
2. Look for a family therapist just like you would a family primary care doctor.
3. Every time you lock your door at night, ask yourself, "Am I putting my mental health protection in place?"

QUESTIONS FOR REFLECTION AND DISCUSSION

1. Have you ever talked to a therapist? If so, what was the motivation? If not, why not?

2. How do you deal with failure?
3. What is your defense mechanism when you feel emotional pain?
4. How are you protecting your peace of mind and mental health?

10

CLARITY

HOW WE MADE IT OVER

*Let us hold unswervingly to the hope we
profess, for he who promised is faithful.*

Hebrews 10:23

After years of struggle, years of tears, and years of preaching faith, while struggling with my own, the faithfulness of God penetrated the dark days and literally turned them into blue skies. It began with the unscrupulous lending institution that illegally harassed us and didn't keep their word. A local lender stepped in and conducted underwriting that uncovered the professionalism and strict adherence to the fiduciary responsibility of the financial affairs of the church. They were surprised why so many lending institutions had ignored the obvious. Could it be the color of money is green sometimes?[1]

Without saying words that would libel another institution or throw shade on the lending industry in general, the lender that stepped up implied that it wasn't the color of our money.[2] As we signed documents at the closing table, it was a long-awaited affirmation. We had managed God's money with the highest integrity. We had made the best decisions we could given the unequal field of play.[3]

Then came the blue skies of the construction company. They completed our construction project after the bank walked away. Because the financial institution had misled both of us, the church was left owing money to the construction company. I believed the only right thing to do was to pay them and the mortgage company. When we paid their debts, the vision board and I asked to meet with the principal of the company and their board of directors. I apologized for failing to pay them at the completion of the construction and for their company having to carry our debt on their books, possibly affecting their bond ratings and impacting their business.

The meeting went better than expected. They explained to us they never intended to put a lien against the church, as they believed we had been taken advantage of. They had to exact pressure for us to pay at the advice of their lawyers and auditors. They went on to say they believed in the work we were doing in the community. To hear them say those words brought an unspeakable joy to my soul. All the while I believed my reputation and the narrative of New Life was damaged beyond repair, God was faithful and had given us undisclosed favor. They repeated that from a business point of view they had to do those things, but our reputation preceded us and spoke for us when we were not in the room.

The community narrative had begun to turn, and in some corners, it was never even tarnished. Now I saw the faithfulness of God, and as Elijah heard his still quiet voice, I too was hearing it more clearly. To reach a wider community, I believed our church under its community development corporation arm would start a Boys and Girls club, and incredibly, the construction company owner threw his support behind the idea—the same construction company that we owed due to the financial institution that misrepresented themselves to us and refused to pay for the work. One would have thought that relationship would have been broken beyond repair.

The owner of the company commended our untiring efforts to pay off our debt and reaffirmed his belief that we were abused by the dishonest lending institutions. He assembled business leaders, community leaders, and civic leaders at his membership-only dinner club for an interest meeting. The faithfulness of God gave me favor. As Elijah left the cave, refreshed with angel food, and walked another forty miles to fulfill his mission in life, so did I. I am reminded of the lyrics of The Winans' song "Breaking of Day": "Now I'd been down, so long I could not hear a song. . . . Now I can feel the breaking of day."[4]

RUN ON AND SEE WHAT THE END IS GOING TO BE!

My mother used to tell me, "Son, run on and see what the end is going to be." Clarity! That's what it's going to be. The tide was turning, and the gravitational pull of a church core leadership staying together was producing even more. As the church emerged from the struggles of construction and community damage control, we formed a community development corporation (CDC). The New Life CDC was created to build communities of choice to provide affordable housing for seniors aged fifty-five and older. You would think anyone who had as many setbacks and challenges and constructions as we had would have learned our lesson. We did. We applied every lesson we learned.

The favor of God's faithfulness continues to manifest all around us. It was as if God was saying, "I tested, tried, and put your leadership through the furnace. You came out as pure gold." To whom much is given much is required. This time God quickly assembled a team to lead the community effort to build houses. God sent a developer and reputable banks to fund the project using tax credits. The church was not asked to use our financials or tithes and offerings. The lessons we learned made us credible partners to manage a $20 million affordable housing project.

Clarity

The developer cited our experience, determination following setbacks, integrity, and business acumen as reasons why he wanted to partner with us. The church went from struggling with a $6.5 million church project to managing four times that amount. When you lead little well, God gives you more to lead. Our reputation and influence grew like a seed buried in the darkness of soil. God was giving the increase everywhere we turned. The future residual income and developer fees that NLC CDC would pay strategically positioned the church to institutionalize itself in the community.

I am convinced God would not have brought these opportunities to me had I given up. God needed to see that I could endure. He said in 1 Corinthians 10:13 that he "is faithful; he will not let you be tempted beyond what you can bear. But when you are tempted, he will also provide a way out so that you can endure it." The endurance of my leadership had equipped me for what he had for me. God didn't stop with restructuring, our Boys and Girls club initiative, or the housing project. God established us as a minority developer, positioning NLC CDC to do projects nationwide. Our reach has made it with two major projects all the way to North Carolina. Then God gave us favor with Southern Illinois University Edwardsville to house their Head Start program. They even named it New Life Head Start, not knowing we had attempted to have our own preschool daycare years earlier. It had come full circle now.

God continues to speak to me after rain has stopped and the skies are blue. Once I made up in my mind that I needed to follow my executive coach's advice, I began to dream again. The vision for the church began to come even more alive. We had started building a youth building on our campus but had to stop when the sanctuary projects resumed. It began to bubble up in my spirit to restart this project. But how? Timing is everything and taking on another construction project seemed a bit much.

We needed financial partners. I learned through my partnerships with the university that when organizations have like values, partnership produces amazing things. With that in mind, I reached out to Southern Illinois Health Foundation (SIHF) to help complete the Charles and Deanne Rayford Family Development Center, which would be the youth building. We had started building it as a pay-as-we-go project, but it became a casualty of the many storms. So, for years it was finished on the outside waiting for a buildout.

SIHF helped fund the redesign of the building to bring it up to code in exchange for square footage to provide behavioral health to our church and community. The pandemic exposed the need for mental health within and without our church. Our contractor services were able to partner with this foundation to use our unfinished youth building for a fee, helping the church finish the building. Again, endurance had produced God's trust in us to lead more. The favor of God was breaking out all around us. I can see clearly now. All obstacles that weren't removed became manageable. The remaining obstacles were and are being maneuvered around with crucible-burnished-and-built leadership skills.

THE TEST OF TIME

"But he knows every detail of what is happening to me; and when he has examined me, he will pronounce me completely innocent—as pure as solid gold!" (Job 23:10 TLB). There were so many times I felt like Job in the testing of my faith. Just as Job had friends to tell him he must have done something wrong for all the things going wrong in his life, there were times when I heard the same from some in the community and the congregation. Leadership can be extremely lonely at times. Having the stamina to withstand criticism takes the strong leadership of Job. The determination of one's body is not always visible when a leader is leading against all odds of success.

The deterioration of one's body is internal, and I, like Job, had to wait until my change came.

The public discourse Job had to have with friends who confronted him with their opinions about his problems now became public fodder. This discourse also put Job's leadership on display. Leaders don't always have the luxury of having private skin sores, sickness almost unto death, or deliberate testing by God. Leaders' pains more often than not become public by default, design, or unintentionally. But if the leader can hold out a reward, more awaits them—many times equal to the pain. I remember the words of my spiritual mentor: "The level of your leadership is commensurate to the level of your pain when you are willing to endure."

Job received more, and so did I. "And the Lord restored the fortunes of Job, when he had prayed for his friends. And the Lord gave Job twice as much as he had before" (Job 42:10 ESV). The mantle of leadership has a price tag attached to it by God, and the lure of leadership sets one up to be seduced into it by God, taking on the weight of God's work he has assigned to me. Reflecting on this brought to mind advice I received from my spiritual mentor. Jeremiah testifies to this paradoxical relationship between God, the leader, their responsibility, and the frailty of the leader's desire to lead. "If you have raced with men on foot, and they have wearied you, how will you compete with horses? And if in a safe land you are so trusting, what will you do in the thicket of the Jordan?" (Jeremiah 12:5 ESV); "O Lord, you have deceived me, and I was deceived; you are stronger than I, and you have prevailed. I have become a laughingstock all the day; everyone mocks me" (Jeremiah 20:7 ESV). Receiving more came at a cost in an even bigger reward. Jeremiah's weighty call to leadership cost him quite a lot of anguish but his reward was the fulfillment of carrying out his assignment.

LESSONS LEARNED

I learned so much about leadership that takes me back to that young overconfident teenager who preached his initial sermon to a standing-room-only crowd. If I knew this awaited my zeal to lead, I would have had a little talk with myself. I would have told that zealous eighth grader that the birth of the law of leadership stiffens your back. I would've told myself to make sure my zeal was equal to my endurance. I would have warned that the shouts of amens and hallelujahs from a crowd at church can turn into silence and recrimination. I would have said that as fast and as far away a crowd would drive to see you rise, it would also turn into leaving as fast in the opposite direction.

I would tell myself to hold onto the core relationships because crowds and community accolades come and go and the applause needs to be replaced with the still, quiet voice of God in a lonely cave somewhere off the beaten path. I would encourage a deep devotion to prayer and solitude because it prepares a leader for what they will inevitably face. I would say that not everybody will not see you as a failure even when you have failed, and integral relationships will pay off in the end. I would tell myself that sleepless nights will eventually turn into joy in the morning, because if you give up in the darkness of your night, you will not see how God was going to bring you out.

LEADERSHIP PRINCIPLES

The leadership principle that emerged in the moment of clarity was authentic leadership. Authentic leaders are determined to better themselves with each victory and defeat. The cost of leadership causes them to be more self-aware. What emerges is a more disciplined leader. Their ability to focus causes them to be even more driven toward outcomes.[5] Authentic leaders have a deep sense of unwavering faith that the vision and mission will be accomplished some way or the other. Their anchor and internal north star help to keep the organization together, and their faith that it will is a gravitational pull to followers.[6] Elijah, Job, and Jeremiah exemplified moments of faith that prepared them for what was to come.

The transparency of authentic leaders draws followers into following through tough times.[7] They have the ability to be aware of their emotions and understand how emotions affect others.[8] It is self-evident in the culture that is absorbed with reality TV, the appetite for leaders who are real and not carbon copies of what they think people want them to be causes loyalty to increase—even when the organization is challenged.[9] I saw this firsthand. The church rose to meet the challenges. One of the colloquialisms of the church has become, "God called us to do the hard things." Indeed, we did the hard thing and God richly rewarded us with more influence, more projects, and more opportunities to save more souls and change more lives.

FINAL WORDS

Paul said he poured himself out like a drink offering for those God had called him to serve (Philippians 2:17). He said on another occasion he had become all things to all men so that he might save some (1 Corinthians 9:22). I would characterize my efforts in this book in that way. I attempted to pour myself out in order to help ministry leaders save some. Ministry is not easy even though it looked that way to me as a know-it-all youngster preaching his trial sermon. My best friend at the time thought we knew everything one needed to know about ministry. Years later I tried to share the little I know through the broken clay pot of my life. Here are some final points of encouragement for you:

1. I hope you have learned, in part, how to be authentic in your leadership. Inauthentic leaders are fragile and easily break under pressure.

2. Do your best to develop your followers. Paul told the church at Philippi that he was happy some obeyed him in his absence even when others only cared about themselves and ignored his leadership from prison.

3. Prayer and consecration are critical. Your spirit must be free from distraction when the winds of life and storms of ministry come—and they will come. They will come hitting the shoreline of ministry when you least expect it. Consecrate yourself with daily quiet time.

4. Embrace therapy. It will help you balance your life. To date I struggle with balancing my life, I struggle with acceptance and rejection, and I struggle with fear of failure and public shame. Here is the difference from the start of my ministry until now: therapy helped me to recognize these issues from afar and pray for the courage and strength to overcome them when they arise. These issues try to overcome me—and they fail every time.

5. If your budget can manage therapy and executive coaching, take advantage of them. Mentors can help if executive coaching is budget prohibitive. Remember, Jesus walked on water, and you can't. Even Peter found out he couldn't. Also remember Jesus died for the church, so you don't have to. The job of Savior has already been taken and it's a one-deep position.

6. Walk by faith and not by sight. Take measured risks, but don't over promise because you cannot guarantee outcomes and you will underdeliver. Since you will, make sure you manage expectations of yourself and your congregation.

7. Be patient. When tribulation comes, let patience have its perfect work (James 1:2-3). Never forget ministry is a long game, and you are but a handful of years in God's continuum of kingdom time. Kingdom time will keep running until we get to eternal

time. Your lifespan is just a part of God's plan for the church you lead—not the whole plan.

8. Try your best not to build a church building and the people at the same time. Plant the church first, build the building afterward. If you have no choice, build your core and framework first. Maintain your integrity and don't chase good or bad narratives about your ministry and leadership. Focus on the vision and not what the peanut gallery is saying. Corrie ten Boom said she takes all the compliments she receives and puts them in a vase at the end of the day to give to Jesus. Follow her advice.

9. Pursue formal training and development. Seminary education is as needed as the surgeon going into the operating room. If you do not have the resources to go to seminary, do your best to better yourself through conferences and informal training. Preparation for a life of ministry is a life poured out like a drink offering every day then turning to Jesus to fill you back up!

Leadership has a playbook for every leadership opportunity you enter in. The playbook is comprised of biblical principles, well researched leadership theory, experiences, and you writing your story in real time. Each opportunity will present itself with a chance to win one for the team or wrestle defeat from the jaws of victory. But no matter the outcome, it is not a failure but an opportunity to learn how to lead in the midst of a storm.

QUESTIONS FOR REFLECTION AND DISCUSSION

1. Can you recall a time when you almost gave up? What caused you to hold on?
2. Have there been times in your life when you have given up?
3. How do you recognize clarity of purpose in your life?

ACKNOWLEDGMENTS

Nothing gets done without someone helping you and nothing great happens by someone acting on their own. So it is with this book. I am so thankful for the faith my parents taught me, Bishop Leamon Dudley Sr., DD, and Ida Dorothy Dudley; both are with the Lord. They have already written and read this book through the years they raised me and encouraged me to do great things. My mother use to tell me, "Son, you will preach to thousands." I can only hope thousands read this book. My father bragged unashamedly to his denomination colleagues about what God was doing through my life. Daddy, I believe this book will make you proud.

I want to thank my family, Glenda, Mahogany (Travis), and Geoffrey II, who have shared me with ministry. This book is a turning point for me. It has opened my eyes to how I need to do a better job with balancing ministry with family. Thanks for your patience!

The staff of New Life in Christ is unbeatable. Dagne for typing, editing, and suggestions. Vivian, your business acumen and loyalty are next to none. Jermaine, it's the worship that helped me. Ashton's wit and work. Jessica's effervescent presence. Daria's smile and personality that greet every LifeChanger. Matthew's number crunching and stick-to-itiveness. Dr. Ken's (DK) attention to detail.

You carry me from one Sunday to the next. You deserve all the accolades I get because I stand on your shoulders for every book, sermon, Bible study, community meeting, and leadership event. Also Dr. Michael Emerson who, after we talked about my journey, encouraged me to write this book and suggested I contact InterVarsity Press and submit a proposal.

I would be remiss if I did not thank my editor, Nilwona Nowlin; my writing coach, Regina; and the entire InterVarsity Press team who believed my story was worth publishing.

New Life leadership: vision board, elders, ministers, deacons, pastoral ministry leaders, helps ministry leaders, and LifeChanger covenant partners—without you, as John Maxwell said, "If you think you are a leader and you look behind you and don't see anyone, you are just taking a walk."[1] When I look behind me, I see you following me as I follow Christ through the storms and sunshiny days. THANK YOU.

APPENDIX
SELF-ASSESSMENT TOOLS

- Colors Personality Test: https://mypersonality.net/quiz
- Strengths Finder Assessment: www.gallup.com/cliftonstrengths/en/strengthsfinder.aspx
- Values Assessment: https://personalvalu.es
- Enneagram Personality Assessment: https://enneagramtest.com
- Spiritual Gifts Assessment: https://giftstest.com

NOTES

1. CALLING

[1] Simon Sinek, *Start with Why: How Great Leaders Inspire Everyone to Take Action* (New York: Portfolio Penguin, 2009).

[2] Myles Monroe, *In Pursuit of Purpose* (Shippensburg, PA: Destiny Image Publishers, 1992).

[3] Eric Geiger and Kevin Peck, *Designed to Lead: The Church and Leadership Development* (Nashville, TN: B&H Publishing, 2016).

[4] Erik D. Salwen, et al., "Self-Disclosure and Spiritual Well-Being in Pastors Seeking Professional Psychological Help," *Pastoral Psychology* 66, no. 4 (April 2017): 505-21, https://doi.org/10.1007/s11089-017-0757-1.

[5] Robert C. Rogers and Taunya M. Tinsley, "Black Pastors' Experiences of Occupational and Life Stress During COVID-19 in the USA," *Journal of Religion and Health* 63, no. 1 (August 2023): 685-703, https://doi.org/10.1007/s10943-023-01901-9.

[6] Andrew J. Weaver, et al., "Mental Health Issues Among Clergy and Other Religious Professionals: A Review of Research," *Journal of Pastoral Care and Counseling* 56, no. 4 (February 2002): 393-403, https://doi.org/10.1177/154230500205600408.

[7] Douglas Miller, "My Soul Has Been Anchored in the Lord," *Unspeakable Joy*, Light Records, 1985.

[1] Geoffrey Vincent Dudley, "Planting Growing Churches in the 21st Century" (DMin project, School of Theology, Virginia Union University, 2000).

[2] Richard J. Krejcir, "Statistics on Pastors," Church Leadership, 2007, www.churchleadership.org/apps/articles/default.asp?blogid=0&view=post&articleid=42347&contentonly=true.

[3] Tony Morgan, "Mental Health—Episode 80," in The Unstuck Church Podcast, https://theunstuckgroup.com/mental-health-episode-80-the-unstuck-church-podcast/.

[4] Josh Packard and Ashleigh Hope, *Church Refugees: Sociologists Reveal Why People Are DONE with Church but Not Their Faith* (Loveland, CO: Group, 2015).

[5] "Pastors Share Top Reasons They've Considered Quitting Ministry in the Past Year," Barna, April 27, 2022, www.barna.com/research/pastors-quitting-ministry.

[6] Peter G. Northouse, *Leadership: Theory and Practice*, 7th ed. (Thousand Oaks, CA: Sage, 2016), 196.

2. CORE

[1] Matt Williams, "The Sun," Phys.org, September 28, 2015, https://phys.org/news/2015-09-sun.html.

[2] Geoffrey V. Dudley Sr., "Leader-Member Exchange in Matthew 17:1-23 and Jesus Developing High-Exchange Relationships (In-Groups and Out-Groups) and Leadership Development (DMin diss., School of Theology, Virginia Union University, 2019), 8.

[3] Dudley, "Leader-Member Exchange," 102.

3. CONSECRATED COURAGE

[1] James Cleveland, "Peace Be Still," by James Cleveland, Savoy Records, 1963.

[2] Sun Tzu, *The Art of War*, trans. Lionel Giles (Mineola, NY: Dover, 2002), originally published in China around the fifth century BC.

[3] Glen G. Scorgie, ed., *Dictionary of Christian Spirituality* (Grand Rapids, MI: Zondervan, 2011), 49.

[4] Peter G. Northouse, *Leadership: Theory and Practice*, 7th ed. (Thousand Oaks, CA: Sage, 2016), 93.

4. CONSTRUCTION

[1] "Stress Symptoms: Effects on Your Body and Behavior," Healthy Lifestyle, Mayo Clinic, August 10, 2023, www.mayoclinic.org/healthy-lifestyle/stress-management/in-depth/stress-symptoms/art-20050987.

[2] Geoffrey Vincient Dudley, "Planting Growing Churches in the 21st Century" (DMin project, School of Theology, Virginia Union University, 2000).

[3] Dasha Grajfoner, Celine Rojon, and Farjam Eshraghian, "Academic Leaders: In-role Perceptions and Developmental Approaches," *Educational Management Administration & Leadership* 52, no. 5 (August 17, 2022), https://doi.org/10.1177/17411432221095957.

[4] Dudley, "Planting Growing Churches."

[5] Reid Hoffman and Ben Casnocha, *The Startup of You: Adapt to the Future, Invest in Yourself, and Transform Your Career* (New York: Random House, 2012), 83.

[6] Michael Jordan and Mark Vancil, *I Can't Accept Not Trying: Michael Jordan on the Pursuit of Excellence* (San Francisco, CA: Harper San Francisco, 1994).
[7] Pat Summitt, *Reach for the Summit: The Definite Dozen* (New York: Broadway Books, 1999), 173.

5. CANCELED

[1] Dictionary.com, Pop Culture Dictionary, s.v. "cancel culture," July 31, 2020, www.dictionary.com/e/pop-culture/cancel-culture/.
[2] Brian Jones, "The #1 Secret of Church Growth," Senior Pastor Central, accessed July 30, 2024, https://seniorpastorcentral.com/918/1-secret-church-growth/.
[3] Peter J. O'Connor, et al., "Leader Tolerance of Ambiguity: Implications for Follower Performance Outcomes in High and Low Ambiguous Work Situations," *The Journal of Applied Behavioral Science* 58, no. 3 (November 2021): 65-96, https://doi.org/10.1177/00218863211053676.
[4] Gary Chapman, *The Five Love Languages: How to Express Heartfelt Commitment to Your Mate* (Farmington Hills, MI: Walker, 2010).

6. CHAOS

[1] Sapan Saxena, *Finders, Keepers* (Mumbai, India: Frog Books, 2015), 193.
[2] John S. Bums, "Chaos Theory and Leadership Studies: Exploring Uncharted Seas," *Journal of Leadership & Organizational Studies* 9, no. 2 (September 2002): 42, https://doi.org/10.1177/107179190200900204.
[3] Elizabeth Korver-Glenn, et al., "Displaced and Unsafe: The Legacy of Settler-Colonial Racial Capitalism in the U.S. Rental Market," *Journal of Race, Ethnicity and the City* 4, no. 1 (February 2023): 113-34, https://doi.org/10.1080/26884674.2023.2176799; Emily E. Lynch, et al., "The Legacy of Structural Racism: Associations Between Historic Redlining, Current Mortgage Lending, and Health," *SSM - Population Health* 14 (June 2021), https://doi.org/10.1016/j.ssmph.2021.100793.
[4] Korver-Glenn, "Displaced and Unsafe," 2.
[5] Korver-Glenn, "Displaced and Unsafe," 2.
[6] Junia Howell and Elizabeth Korver-Glenn, "Neighborhoods, Race, and the Twenty-First-Century Housing Appraisal Industry," *Sociology of Race and Ethnicity* 4, no. 4 (February 2018): 1, https://doi.org/10.1177/2332649218755178.
[7] Howell, "Neighborhoods," 1.
[8] Bernard M. Bass and Bruce J. Avolio, introduction to *Improving Organizational Effectiveness Through Transformational Leadership*, ed. Bernard M. Bass and Bruce J. Avolio (Thousand Oaks, CA: Sage, 1991), 3.
[9] Bass and Avolio, introduction to *Improving Organizational Effectiveness*, 3-4.

[10] Bruce J. Avolio, "The Alliance of Total Quality and the Full Range of Leadership" in *Improving Organizational Effectiveness*.

7. CASH

[1] If you're not familiar with the concept of redlining, these are helpful resources: Michael O. Emerson, "Residential Segregation Rewards Whites While Punishing People of Color," *Urban Edge*, September 21, 2020, https://kinder.rice.edu/urbanedge/residential-segregation-rewards-whites-while-punishing-people-color; Elizabeth Korver-Glenn, *Race Brokers* (New York: Oxford University Press, 2021); Junia Howell and Elizabeth Korver-Glenn, "The Increasing Effect of Neighborhood Racial Composition on Housing Values, 1980–2015," *Social Problems* 68, no. 1: 1051-71, https://doi.org/10.1093/socpro/spaa033; Kristen Broady, Mac McComas, and Amine Ouazad, "An Analysis of Financial Institutions in Black-Majority Communities: Black Borrowers and Depositors Face Considerable Challenges in Accessing Banking Services," Brookings, November 2, 2021, www.brookings.edu/articles/an-analysis-of-financial-institutions-in-black-majority-communities-black-borrowers-and-depositors-face-considerable-challenges-in-accessing-banking-services/.

[2] Heather McGhee, *The Sum of Us: What Racism Costs Everyone and How We Can Prosper Together* (New York: One World, 2022), xvii; Howell and Korver-Glenn, "Neighborhoods, Race, and the Twenty-First-Century Housing Appraisal Industry," 1.

[3] Elizabeth Korver-Glenn, et al., "Displaced and Unsafe: The Legacy of Settler-Colonial Racial Capitalism in the U.S. Rental Market," *Journal of Race, Ethnicity and the City* 4, no. 1 (February 2023): 113-34, https://doi.org/10.1080/26884674.2023.2176799.

[4] Korver-Glenn, "Displaced and Unsafe," 113-34.

[5] Emerson, "Residential Segregation Rewards Whites While Punishing People of Color"; Korver-Glenn, *Race Brokers*; Howell and Korver-Glenn, "The Increasing Effect of Neighborhood Racial Composition on Housing Values, 1980-2015"; Kristen Broady, Mac McComas, and Amine Ouazad, "An Analysis of Financial Institutions in Black-Majority Communities," November 2, 2021, Brookings, www.brookings.edu/articles/an-analysis-of-financial-institutions-in-black-majority-communities-black-borrowers-and-depositors-face-considerable-challenges-in-accessing-banking-services/.

[6] Nikole Hannah-Jones, *The 1619 Project: A New Origin Story* (New York: One World, 2019), 337-39.

[7] Malcolm Gladwell, *The Tipping Point* (New York: Little, Brown, 2006), 342.

[8] Michael Evans, David McFadden, and Michael O. Emerson, *Kingdom Racial Change: Overcoming Inequality, Injustice, and Indifference* (Grand Rapids, MI: Eerdmans, 2025); Korver-Glenn, *Race Brokers*.

[9] Pamela Foohey, "Lender Discrimination, Black Churches, and Bankruptcy," *Houston Law Review* 54, no. 5 (May 2017): 1079, https://houstonlawreview.org/article/3938.

[10] Foohey, "Lender Discrimination," 1079; Emily E. Lynch, et al., "The Legacy of Structural Racism: Associations Between Historic Redlining, Current Mortgage Lending, and Health," *SSM - Population Health* 14 (June 2021), https://doi.org/10.1016/j.ssmph.2021.100793.

[11] McGhee, *The Sum of Us*, xvii.

[12] Foohey, "Lender Discrimination," 1079.

[13] Peter G. Northouse, *Leadership: Theory and Practice*, 7th ed. (Thousand Oaks, CA: Sage, 2016), 227-29.

[14] Northouse, *Leadership*, 227-29.

8. COMMUNITY

[1] Lichuan Liu, et al., "Infant Cry Language Analysis and Recognition: An Experimental Approach," *IEEE/CAA Journal of Automatica Sinica* 6, no. 3 (May 2019): 778-88, https://doi.org/10.1109/JAS.2019.1911435.

[2] Peter G. Northouse, *Leadership: Theory and Practice*, 7th ed. (Thousand Oaks, CA: Sage, 2016), 78-79.

9. COUNSELING

[1] Ingrid M. Erickson, "Fighting Fire with Fire: Jane Elliott's Antiracist Pedagogy," *Counterpoints* 240 (2004): 145-57, www.jstor.org/stable/42978385; *The Eye of the Storm*, directed by William Peters (New York: ABC News, 1970).

[2] Janice Bell Meisenhelder and Emily N. Chandler, "Frequency of Prayer and Functional Health in Presbyterian Pastors," *Journal for the Scientific Study of Religion* 40, no. 2 (December 2002): 323-30, https://www.jstor.org/stable/1387954.

[3] Deanna Doss Shrodes, "The Prevalence of Unaddressed Trauma in the Lives of Ministerial Leaders and Pastoral Care-Oriented Steps to Greater Spiritual and Emotional Health," (PhD diss., Southeastern University, 2022), iii.

[4] Jill Anne Hendron, Pauline Irving, and Brian Taylor, "The Unseen Cost: A Discussion of the Secondary Traumatization Experience of the Clergy," *Pastoral Psychology* 61 (2012): 221-31, https://doi.org/10.1007/s11089-011-0378-z.

[5] Geoffrey Dudley Sr., "Online Lesson on Self-Leadership," February 2023, https://www.ileadacademy.net.

⁶ Travis Bradberry and Jean Greaves, *Emotional Intelligence 2.0* (San Diego: TalentSmart, 2009).
⁷ Dudley, "Online Lesson on Self-Leadership."

10. CLARITY

¹ Michael Evans, David McFadden, and Michael O. Emerson, *Kingdom Racial Change: Overcoming Inequality, Injustice, and Indifference* (Grand Rapids, MI: Eerdmans, 2025, forthcoming); Elizabeth Korver-Glenn, *Race Brokers* (New York: Oxford University Press, 2021).
² Evans et al., *Kingdom Racial Change*; Korver-Glenn, *Race Brokers*.
³ Evans et al., *Kingdom Racial Change*; Korver-Glenn, *Race Brokers*.
⁴ Marvin Winans, "Breaking of Day," The Winans, *Decisions* (Qwest Records, 1987).
⁵ Bruce J. Avolio and William L. Gardner, "Authentic Leadership Development: Getting to the Root of Positive Forms of Leadership," *The Leadership Quarterly* 16, no. 3 (June 2005): 315-38, https://doi.org/10.1016/j.leaqua.2005.03.001.
⁶ Avolio and Gardner, "Authentic Leadership Development," 315-38.
⁷ Peter G. Northouse, *Leadership: Theory and Practice*, 7th ed. (Thousand Oaks, CA: Sage, 2016), 195.
⁸ Jean Greaves and Travis Bradberry, *Emotional Intelligence 2.0* (San Diego: TalentSmart, 2009).
⁹ William L. Gardner, Bruce J. Avolio, and Fred O. Walumbwa, "Authentic Leadership Development: Emergent Themes and Future Directions," in *Authentic Leadership Theory and Practice: Origins, Effects and Development*, Monographs in Leadership and Management 3 (Bingley, UK: Emerald, 2005), 387-406.

ACKNOWLEDGMENTS

¹ John C. Maxwell, *Developing the Leader Within You* (Nashville, TN: Thomas Nelson, 2005), 78.

Like this book?
Scan the code to discover more content like this!

Get on IVP's email list to receive special offers, exclusive book news, and thoughtful content from your favorite authors on topics you care about.

IVPRESS.COM/BOOK-QR